It Happened In Alabama

It Happened In Alabama

Remarkable Events That Shaped History

Jackie Sheckler Finch

Guilford, Connecticut

Project editor: Meredith Dias
Layout: Kevin Mak
Map: Daniel Lloyd © 2011 by Morris Publishing, LLC

Library of Congress Cataloging-in-Publication Data
Finch, Jackie Sheckler, 1942-
  It happened in Alabama / Jackie Sheckler Finch.
    p. cm.
  Includes bibliographical references.
  ISBN 978-0-7627-6113-5
  1. Alabama—History—Anecdotes. 2. Alabama—History, Local—Anecdotes. 3. Alabama—Biography—Anecdotes. I. Title.

F326.6.F56 2011
976.1—dc22

2011005418a

Printed in the United States of America

10 9 8 7 6 5 4 3 2 1

This book is dedicated to my family—Kelly Rose; Mike Peters; Sean Rose, Devin, Dylan, and Emma; Stefanie Rose, Will, Trey, and Arianna Scott; and Logan Peters, Miranda, and Olivia.

And to my best travel buddies, Debbie Geiger and Sharyn Kuneman, for all the fantastic times we have had in amazing Alabama.

A special remembrance to my husband, Bill Finch, whose spirit goes with me every mile and step of the way through life's journey.

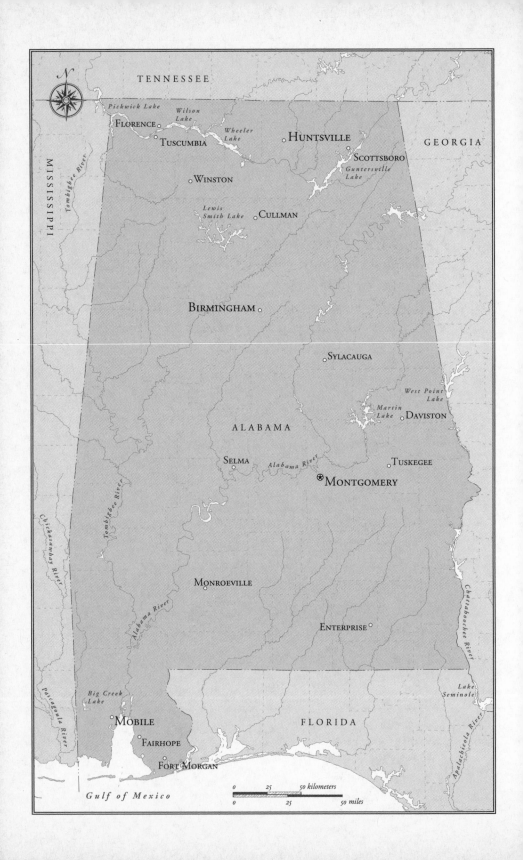

N

TENNESSEE

Pickwick Lake

FLORENCE

Wilson Lake

TUSCUMBIA

Wheeler Lake

HUNTSVILLE

SCOTTSBORO

GEORGIA

WINSTON

Guntersville Lake

Lewis Smith Lake

CULLMAN

MISSISSIPPI

Tombigbee River

BIRMINGHAM

SYLACAUGA

West Point Lake

ALABAMA

Martin Lake

DAVISTON

SELMA

Alabama River

TUSKEGEE

⊛ MONTGOMERY

Tombigbee River

Chickasawhay River

MONROEVILLE

Alabama River

ENTERPRISE

Chattahoochee River

Pascagoula River

Big Creek Lake

Lake Seminole

MOBILE

FAIRHOPE

FLORIDA

Apalachicola River

FORT MORGAN

Gulf of Mexico

0   25   50 kilometers

0   25   50 miles

CONTENTS

CONTENTS

INTRODUCTION

The first time someone told me about an Alabama fishing jubilee, I thought they were pulling my leg. Sort of like the imaginary snipe hunt that my cousin tried to send me on when I was a kid. It sounded too far-fetched to be true.

Fish, shrimp, crabs, and other sea critters crawl, flop, or wobble up on the shore, two old fishermen in Fairhope told me. All you had to do was walk around and pick up the bountiful seafood. Could this possibly be true?

It most certainly is. And it is just one of the many things I love about amazing Alabama. Although jubilees have been reported in other areas, Mobile Bay is probably the only body of water in which this phenomenon occurs fairly regularly, according to the Auburn University Marine Extension and Research Center in Mobile.

It all starts with a phone call from a friend, usually in the middle of the night. The message is relayed with shouts of "Jubilee!" And the fishing is on.

Seems strange to call it fishing. Rather it is gathering. Folks bring out washtubs, sacks, and plastic buckets and fill them up with the high-priced delicacies of the deep. When the sun comes up, all returns to normal.

Jubilees usually end at sunrise when oxygen is produced by the photosynthetic activity of plant life in the water. That's what caused the fish to come to the surface searching for oxygen. For a jubilee to take place, a very specific set of conditions must exist. Those conditions occur only in the summer between June and September, usually in the early morning before sunrise.

The previous day's weather conditions must include an overcast or cloudy day, a gentle wind from the east, and a calm or slick bay surface. Also a rising tide is necessary. A change to a falling tide will stop the jubilee.

It takes a combination of all these conditions to produce the phenomenon. The whole scientific explanation involves oxygen, salty water, fresh river water, wind, and too much plant matter. Fish and shellfish trapped by jubilee conditions behave very strangely. But their behavior is simply an attempt to get enough oxygen to survive.

Since they cannot get the oxygen they need from the water as they normally do, they come ashore and try to get it from the air. When the sun comes up and the oxygen is back to normal, the affected fish and shellfish that haven't been hauled away for dinner tables then swim back to their bottom-water habitat—until the next jubilee.

Unless you stumble on the happening yourself or are one of the lucky ones on a call list to participate, you might not even know a jubilee is taking place. Jubilees probably happen a lot more than people know, the fishermen told me. It's just that no one is around to see them.

Many accounts of the jubilee exist, the oldest dating back to the 1860s. But no one knows for sure how long they have been taking place, maybe since the beginning of Alabama history.

The history of Alabama is filled with interesting twists and turns. In 1519, Spanish explorer Alonso Alvarez de Pineda claimed the honor as the first white man to set foot in Alabama, sailing into what is now Mobile Bay. The first fully documented visit was by explorer Hernando de Soto in 1539. Spaniards called the area La Florida. The English also laid claims to the region north of the Gulf of Mexico, and the French founded a settlement at Fort Louis on the Mobile River in 1702. For the next nine years, this was the French seat of government for New France or Louisiane (Louisiana). In 1711, Fort Louis was abandoned to floods, and settlers rebuilt a fort on higher ground known as Fort Conde. The first European settlement in Alabama, this was the start of present-day Mobile.

In 1819, Alabama became the twenty-second state in the Union. Alabama got its name from the Native Americans who lived here. After the Indian wars and removal of Native Americans, white settlers arrived in large numbers. By the 1830s, almost all of the Native-American tribes in the region were forced to move westward.

Wealthy planters created large cotton plantations that flourished in the fertile Black Belt soil and depended on the labor of African slaves. Thousands of slaves were transported to and sold by slave traders in the state. Before long, cotton production and slave labor were the dominant factors in the new state's economy. Poor white farmers barely made it by with their small subsistence faming. By 1860, African Americans made up 45 percent of the state's population of 964,201.

When sounds of the Civil War began echoing throughout the land, Alabama seceded from the Union and joined the Confederate States of America from 1861 to 1865. Montgomery became the first capital of the Confederacy with Jefferson Davis as president. The state contributed about 120,000 men to the Confederate service, practically all the white male population capable of bearing arms. Uncounted thousands of slaves worked with Confederate troops, cooking and doing laundry, taking care of horses and equipment, and building defensive installations.

About 10,000 slaves escaped and joined the Union army, along with about 2,700 white men. Slaves were freed in 1865. After the Civil War, Alabama and other former Confederate states entered the era of Reconstruction (1875–77), a period during which the Southern states were reorganized. Alabama was readmitted to the Union in 1868.

After Reconstruction ended, most of the Deep South instituted laws and customs known as Jim Crow laws, which strictly segregated blacks and whites. Not surprisingly, in the mid-twentieth century, Alabama—known as "the Heart of Dixie"—was at the center of the American civil rights movement and home to pivotal events such as the Montgomery bus boycott. The civil rights milestone was sparked when a black seamstress, Rosa Parks, refused to give up her seat on a city bus to a white passenger. One of the organizers of the boycott, a young pastor named Martin Luther King Jr., emerged from the action as a national civil rights leader with a commitment to nonviolent resistance.

Following the boycott, tension between blacks and whites continued, resulting in numerous demonstrations and acts of violence throughout Alabama. Members of the white supremacist group, the Ku Klux Klan, set off a bomb in the Sixteenth Street Baptist Church in Birmingham, killing four young girls. Americans were outraged at the bombing, bringing about support for passage of the Civil Rights Act of 1964, which outlawed segregation in schools, public places, and places of employment.

The eyes of America were again on Alabama during the March 1965 Selma-to-Montgomery marches in support of voting rights for blacks. The violence was captured on live national television as hundreds of black and white marchers were met by Alabama state troopers who attacked them with tear gas and nightsticks. Thousands of demonstrators followed, spurring President Lyndon Johnson to call for passage of a new voting rights bill. In August 1965, Congress passed the Voting Rights Act, which banned discriminatory voting practices, which had been used to disenfranchise blacks.

Today Alabama is proud of its progress and works hard to preserve its history and natural beauty. The state is blessed with historians, historical societies, museums, and attractions. Even the smallest towns seem to have groups of people and cubbyhole museums carefully collecting local stories. The twenty-five tales in this book are only a tiny fraction of the fascinating saga of Alabama.

I would especially like to thank the state historians, tourism officials, and other folks who helped me research this book. Gratitude to my Globe Pequot editor, Meredith Rufino, for believing that Alabama is filled with wonderful stories, and to my project editors, Ellen Urban and Meredith Dias, for their keen attention to detail.

So many other stories are waiting to be told. It is an honor that you have chosen this book as your companion in discovering more about Alabama. I sincerely hope it helps guide your steps into making your Alabama historical experience a rewarding and memorable one.

AMERICA'S FIRST MARDI GRAS

1703

After surviving a deadly scourge of yellow fever, a colony of French soldiers in Mobile decided to celebrate life. Painting their faces red, they feasted and drank. There is no historical record that they paraded. But this festive gathering has gone down in history as the first Mardi Gras celebration in America, a century before Alabama became a state. Today it remains an important part of Alabama Gulf Coast culture.

Mardi Gras is French for "Fat Tuesday," the day before Ash Wednesday. Fat Tuesday comes from the ancient tradition of feasting upon a fat calf on the day before Lent starts in the weeks prior to Easter Sunday. The idea of parading comes from leading an ox through the streets of Paris to remind people not to eat meat during Lent.

It was not until years later, in 1830, that the parade part became popular in Mobile. On New Year's Day, a cotton broker named Michael Krafft and some of his friends gathered up some cowbells, rakes, and hoes in a local hardware store. They then proceeded to march through the streets of Mobile and called themselves the Cow-bellion de Rakin Society.

They liked it so much that the Cowbellions decided to have an annual event tied into Mardi Gras. Some of this partying group carried their customs to New Orleans. In 1857, the Cowbellion de Rakins assisted the Big Easy in setting up a mystic society of its own, the Mystic Krewe of Comus, to this day New Orleans's most prestigious Mardi Gras society.

Mobile festivities grew until the Civil War when celebrations were put aside. Even after the war, Mobile was under Union occupation, and no one felt like partying.

That's when Joseph Stillwell Cain decided that people needed to be happy, and he was going to do something about it. On Shrove Tuesday in 1866, town clerk Cain dressed up in Indian regalia, called himself "Chief Slacabormorinico," and climbed aboard a coal wagon he had decorated. The defiant Cain rode his mule-powered one-float parade through the streets of Mobile, and single-handedly brought about the rebirth of Mardi Gras festivities to the depressed city.

By the time Cain died at age seventy-two, he had founded a number of mystic societies, including the well-known Order of Myths. At Mobile's historic Church Street Cemetery, Cain's tombstone notes: HERE LIES JOE CAIN, THE HEART AND SOUL OF MARDI GRAS IN MOBILE.

Every year on the Sunday before Mardi Gras, the Joe Cain Parade pays honor to the rebel. A "people's parade," the Joe Cain Parade is not filled with big floats. Instead, it is a time to decorate a jalopy, wagon, wheelbarrow, or bicycle and join the parade. Of course, there are always plenty of "Cain's widows" in the processional, weeping and wailing for their man.

Many other balls and parades take place during Mobile's Mardi Gras. Each event is sponsored by a different mystic society, and each tries to out-do each other with elaborately decorated floats. Queens and kings and attendants are chosen for each mystic order, and their extravagant outfits cost thousands of dollars. With about thirty parading societies, or crewes, sometimes there are not enough days in the calendar for all the parades, so the processionals might have to double up with two parading in one day, back to back.

Names of the mystics include the Knights of Revelry, Mystical Ladies, Maids of Mirth, Polka Dots, Krewe of Merry Mates, Order of Dragons, and Comic Cowboys. The oldest parading society in Mobile is the Order of Myths, founded in 1867. Its emblem consists of Folly chasing Death around the broken pillar of life, a symbol of Mardi Gras in Mobile. The high point of the Mardi Gras season is the coronation of King Felix and his queen, selected from debutantes and gentlemen of society, often passing from generation to generation. The candidates for king and queen must be unmarried, with the queen usually age nineteen to twenty-two, and the king age twenty-one to twenty-four. As part of the honor, the new king and queen must pay for their costly costumes. Individually designed and handmade, some of the gowns cost $50,000 and up.

As the symbol of Mardi Gras, beaded necklaces are everywhere. Tons of trinkets are tossed out as parade floats glide down the street. Along with necklaces are such flying treats as souvenir cups, candy, toys, stuffed animals, fake doubloons, and, a favorite, moon pies. The soft cookie marshmallow "pies"—shaped like a big round moon—can be thrown long distances without hurting on impact. Mardi Gras colors symbolize purple for justice, green for faith, and gold for power.

The King Cake is a sweet tradition savored during Mardi Gras. The first week of January starts the King Cake season. The original King Cake was associated with Epiphany, January 6, also known as Twelfth Night, when English and Europeans celebrated Christmas for twelve days up to this night. Resembling a coffee cake, the King Cake is oblong, braided, and iced with simple icing sprinkled with purple, green, and gold sugar. Inside each cake is a tiny plastic baby doll, hidden after the cake is baked. According to custom, whoever finds the doll must either buy the next King Cake or throw the next King Cake party.

It is said that Mobile has two seasons—B.C. (before Carnival), when everyone is getting ready for the big event, and D.C. (during Carnival), when folks are concerned with nothing other than celebrating it. When Hurricane Katrina hit the Gulf Coast on August 28 and 29 in 2005, many parts of Mobile were flooded by the intense storm surge. Downtown Mobile was covered with floodwater, mud, and debris, but the parade routes were cleared, and Mobile had the largest Mardi Gras in its history four months later. Attendance was estimated at 878,000. The rallying cry of *Laissez les bon temps roulez* means "let the good times roll."

The once-a-year merriment is a welcome break from reality, celebrants say. As a quotation from the Order of Myths notes, "A little nonsense now and then is relished by the wisest men."

BATTLE OF HORSESHOE BEND

1814

On a quiet spring morning, cannon fire broke the stillness along a lovely spot known as Horseshoe Bend. For two hours, the bombardment led by a hard-fighting general blasted the Indian fortification.

Inside the barricade, the Indians shouted at the soldiers to fight them in hand-to-hand combat. Only a third of the one thousand warriors defending the fort had a musket or rifle. By day's end, most of the warriors lay dead.

The March 27, 1814, Battle of Horseshoe Bend was a major step on a journey that would culminate in the "Trail of Tears" for the Creek Indian Nation and propel frontier General Andrew Jackson into the office of president of the United States. In a peace treaty signed after the battle, the Creeks ceded nearly 23 million acres of land to the United States, paving the way for thousands of American settlers to pour into the vast area, with much of the land becoming the state of Alabama in 1819.

Today the battlefield is preserved by the National Park Service as the 2,040-acre Horseshoe Bend National Military Park, near

Daviston, Alabama. Never before or since in the history of our country have so many American Indians lost their lives in a single battle. It was the final battle of the Creek War of 1813–14.

Before the Battle of Horseshoe Bend, the Creeks—also known as the Muskogee—lived in towns along the rivers of Alabama and Georgia. When settlers began arriving in the area, they called the Creeks who lived along the upper river the Upper Creeks and those along the lower rivers the Lower Creeks.

In 1811, Shawnee military leader Tecumseh visited the tribes hoping to persuade them to return to their ancient traditions and to drive the outsiders from their ancestral lands. Many of the Upper Creeks agreed with Tecumseh. When the War of 1812 started between America and Great Britain, some Creek warriors joined Tecumseh and the British in fighting the Americans.

That set the stage for the Creek Civil War or Creek War of 1813–14 in which Indian factions friendly to Americans fought with Indian factions who were hostile to Americans. Located mostly in the Upper Towns, the Creeks who were anti-Americans were called the Red Sticks, perhaps because they carried red-painted war clubs.

The animosity escalated on July 27, 1813, when a group of Red Sticks was attacked returning from Pensacola with supplies. Ambushed at Burnt Corn Creek, the small Indian force was slaughtered. In retaliation, the Red Sticks attacked a stockade north of Mobile known as Fort Mims on August 30, killing 250 men, women, and children. The Fort Mims massacre brought cries of public outrage.

U.S. authorities sent three armies to converge on the Creek Nation in response to the Fort Mims atrocity. Two of the armies turned back after losses of men and supplies in significant battles. The third army, however, refused to quit, mainly because its leader, Andrew Jackson, was determined to persevere. Renowned for his toughness, the

Tennessee Indian fighter was nicknamed "Old Hickory" because he was as sturdy as an old hickory tree.

Slowing pushing their way south through the mountain and hill country of Alabama, Jackson and his men fought a series of major battles with Red Stick warriors. Reinforced by the 39th U.S. Infantry, Jackson marched on the primary Red Stick fortifications at Tohopeka or Horseshoe Bend in March of 1814.

Designed of heavy logs zigzagged across the narrow neck of the river, the Creek wall was a formidable obstacle. Inside the wall was a temporary village of about three hundred log houses. Across the narrow neck of the bend, the Indians had constructed a log-and-dirt barricade nearly four hundred yards long. The Creeks had hoped their fortified place would protect them from an attacking army or at least delay the attackers while the older men, women, and children escaped downriver.

Living in the barricaded settlement with their women and children, the Creek warriors knew that American troops were marching on their home. Rather than submit to the soldiers, the Indians had decided to fight to the death. In addition to his troops, Jackson also had several hundred Creek and Cherokee warriors who had joined the fight against the Red Sticks. Among them was Sequoya, the explorer and scholar who later invented the Cherokee alphabet.

As March 27 dawned, Jackson sent a large force of Tennessee riflemen led by General John Coffee across the river to surround the fort from the opposite bank. Placing cannons on a steep hill overlooking the Creek barricade, Jackson opened fire on the Indians but soon realized that the Creek fort was too strong. Cannonballs ricocheted off the fort or did little damage if they did make it inside. Deciding to storm the Creek stronghold, Jackson ordered the 39th Infantry and Tennessee militia to attack the Indian fort.

At about the same time, Coffee's troops set fire to the Indian village and attacked the Creek army from the rear. Taking advantage of the diversion, Jackson's men stormed the barricade. Leaping atop the breastwork and shouting for his men to follow, Major Lemuel Montgomery was shot in the head by an Indian bullet and fell lifeless to the ground. The Alabama city of Montgomery was later named in honor of the courageous major. Immediately taking Montgomery's place, Ensign Sam Houston repeated the command. Although an arrow pierced his thigh, Houston ignored the wound and jumped into the compound, followed by a large contingent of soldiers. Houston survived the battle, recovered from his wound, and later went on to fight for Texas independence against Mexico. The Texas city of Houston was named for him.

With American forces attacking on both sides, the outnumbered and outgunned Red Stick warriors were caught in the middle. The battle quickly turned into a brutal massacre. Creek chieftain Menewa was wounded at least seven times and left unconscious among a heap of dead. After dark, he regained consciousness, crawled to the river, found a canoe, and made his escape. Menewa later went west with his people, but there is no record of his life or death in the new country. The end of his life is lost in the annals of history.

As the awful battle raged on the killing field, no quarter was given. None was asked. As Jackson later said, "The carnage was dreadful."

When the battle smoke cleared, the military power of the Creek Nation had been permanently destroyed. About 49 of Jackson's men were killed, another 154 wounded. About 900 warriors were killed. Their 350 or so women and children were taken captive by the Cherokee and Lower Creek warriors.

Houston later described the battle:

The sun was going down, and it set on the ruin of the Creek nation. Where, but a few hours before a thousand brave (warriors) had scowled on death and their assailants, there was nothing to be seen but volumes of dense smoke, rising heavily over the corpses of painted warriors, and the burning ruins of their fortifications.

After Horseshoe Bend, the Creeks were forced to give up the rest of their land in Alabama and relocate to land west of the Mississippi in what is now Oklahoma. The long and deadly march became known as the Trail of Tears.

Jackson went on to defeat the British ten months after Horseshoe Bend at the Battle of New Orleans. Along the way, Jackson became an American hero and ultimately the seventh president of the United States.

THE LAST SLAVE SHIP

1860

When the schooner *Clotilda* set sail from Mobile Bay on March 4, 1860, she looked like any other small cargo ship. But the fast-moving *Clotilda* was heading off to pick up a load of human misery.

The lovely two-masted *Clotilda* has gone down in history as the last known United States slave ship to bring slaves from Africa to America. On her horrific voyage, the *Clotilda* would transport a cargo of enslaved Africans who would go on to build the unusual Africatown just north of Mobile.

Back in 1860, transporting slaves was illegal. A federal law passed by Congress in 1808 prohibited the importing of slaves into America. There weren't supposed to be any more slave ships. But here it was half a century later, and the slave trade was still flourishing. Slaves could fetch a high price in markets, and there were always ship captains and owners willing to break the law. A slave bought in Africa for $50 could easily sell for as much $2,500 in America.

In this particular case, the *Clotilda* was undertaking the perilous trip because her owner, Mobile businessman Timothy Meaher, was said to have bet that he could bring a shipful of slaves into Mobile Bay and sneak them past officials. Meaher hired Captain William Foster to command the ship that would smuggle slaves into the United States.

The stakes were high. Slavers, in theory, could be hanged. Their vessels and cargo could be confiscated. But Meaher wanted to win his wager and get the riches that a shipload of slaves could bring.

On this warm spring day when the *Clotilda* left Mobile Bay, eleven crewmen boarded the vessel, probably not suspecting where they were going or what they were going to do. Sailors didn't like to work on slave ships, not because of any moral compunctions, but because the job was dangerous and dirty. Ship captains often lied about the true nature of a voyage until after the crewmen had signed on or the ship had left port.

But there were telltale signs if anyone had looked carefully.

On board the *Clotilda* were eighty casks of cheap rum, twenty-five boxes of beads and sundries for trading, and $9,000 in gold. Barrels of water and casks of food provisions were far more than the crew needed. In reality, the extra provisions would provide scant sustenance for the Africans that the *Clotilda* expected to transport. Hiding the goods were stacks of lumber that could later be used to build platforms and partitions in the ship's hold where the slaves would be imprisoned.

After a rough journey, the *Clotilda* arrived two and a half months later in Whydah, Africa, on May 15, 1860. Meaher had heard that West African tribes were fighting and that the king of Dahomey was selling captured tribe members into slavery. A slave compound held the captives, as well as criminals condemned to enslavement and kidnap victims—all waiting to be sold. Taking his choice, Foster bought about 125 men, women, and children, often separating the chosen slaves from other family members.

Records show that he chose an equal number of males and females. Although they came from Africa, the captives were from various regions with different cultures, history, religion, and language. Many had never seen white men, the ocean, or the mighty ships that sailed upon the vast waters.

Stripped naked, the slaves were boarded onto the ship but the departure had to be hurried up, and some slaves were left behind on the beach. Foster had seen two steamers approaching and feared they meant to capture his ship. Hauling anchor, the *Clotilda* sailed with about 110 slaves aboard on May 24.

Locked in the hold, which was as hot as a blast furnace, the Africans were kept chained and confined for the first thirteen days as a precaution. When they were finally allowed on deck for the first time, many were unable to stand. Given a swallow of water twice a day, the slaves were tortured by thirst and meager allotments of unfamiliar food. But the *Clotilda* was not plagued with multiple deaths and violence as were most other slave ships. With a smaller than usual load of human cargo, Foster probably wanted to make sure that as many future slaves as possible survived the Middle Passage so that his boss could make a financial killing.

Forty-five days later, the *Clotilda* arrived back in American waters, officially a ship of pirates with a load of contraband. Notified that his slaves had arrived, Meaher arranged for a tugboat to pull the *Clotilda* toward Mobile. Under dead of night, the slave ship made it safely past port officials—or so it seemed.

Alerted to the illegal scheme, federal authorities were waiting. To destroy the evidence, Foster transferred his cargo to a riverboat. Then he burned and sank the *Clotilda.* But the ship didn't go down. Her hull remained visible at low tide northwest of Twelve-Mile Island for three quarters of a century as visible testimony to the hellish deed that had taken place on her.

Given scraps of clothing, the Africans were hidden in swamps and moved from one place to another to escape detection. After about eleven days, the slaves were put on a steamer and moved upriver. But the secret had been revealed. Mobile buzzed with gossip about the deed that Meaher seemed to have pulled off. Although he was arrested for illegally importing slaves and not paying custom taxes on his cargo, Meaher was quickly released and laughed about the incident.

Eager to recoup his investment, Meager arranged a sale of the imported slaves. The Africans later recalled the auction where they were stripped of their clothing, inspected, and bought by various slave masters, as well as being given to two of Meaher's brothers. The largest group of sixteen males and sixteen females became Meaher's property. The community of Africans who had bonded on the ship was now torn apart, literally the loss of a second family and tangible touch of their homeland.

Meaher had won his bet and, in various circles, the ship owner and the ship captain were regarded as heroes for their smuggling exploits. The displaced Africans were forgotten, as though they never existed.

Even the president of the United States, James Buchanan, in delivering his State of the Union Address on December 3, 1860, reported that "since the date of my last annual message not a single slave has been imported into the United States in violation of the laws prohibiting African slave trade."

For six long years, the Africans slaved in servitude while a bloody Civil War split the United States. When the war ended, the slaves were freed. Many of them walked out of the fields and took little or nothing with them. An estimated four million people had been set free. Southern roads were filled with former slaves, many of them looking for family members who had been sold off. Runaways returned from the North, hoping to be reunited with loved ones.

The *Clotilda* Africans on the Meaher brothers' plantations left their masters and decided to reunite with their shipboard family. If they couldn't return to their African homeland, they would create a new Africa in the nation where they had been enslaved.

The men worked in the mills, and the women raised fruits and vegetables until they had saved enough money to buy land from their former slave owners. Settling three miles north of Mobile at Magazine Point, about thirty *Clotilda* Africans built houses, established a church, spoke their own regional language, and adopted their own rules and leaders. An isolated community, the Africans had little contact with whites except on the job.

They named their community Africatown as a proclamation of who they were and where they wanted to be. The town was unique because it was the first time that a group of Africans had built their own town on their own land in the United States. The last survivor of the *Clotilda*, Cudjo Kazoola Lewis, died in 1935 at the age of ninety-four.

Today, Africatown is still home to descendants of the *Clotilda* as well as other African Americans. The log cabins built by their ancestors have been replaced by modern houses, but many of the trees and flowers planted by former *Clotilda* slaves are still flourishing, and the graveyard is the final resting place for the *Clotilda* Africans.

In 1999, the president of Benin (formerly Dahomey) apologized for his country's role in selling as many as three million Africans into slavery. Benin has suffered greatly, he said, from the loss of so many of its own people, called "the absent ones."

FREE STATE OF WINSTON

1861

A summer heat wave sizzled outside a mass meeting at Looney's Tavern on July 4, 1861. But the mood inside the tavern was even hotter. The impending Civil War was the topic under debate and tempers flared.

While the rest of the state was lining up on the side of the Confederacy, the folks of the rugged hill country of northwest Alabama wanted to remain neutral. The poorest county in the state in the 1860s, Winston County wasn't dependent on cotton or slaves. Ninety-eight percent of Winstonians didn't even own a single slave. They saw no need to get involved in the War Between the States.

Back when it was created by the Alabama General Assembly on February 12, 1850, the area was originally named Hancock County for the famed governor of Massachusetts and signer of the Declaration of Independence. The name was changed in 1858 to honor John A. Winston (1812–71), the first governor of Alabama to be born in the state. The earliest settlers to Winston County were independent, hardworking folks from the Carolinas, Georgia, Tennessee, and Virginia.

With poor infertile soil, rugged Winston County was sparsely settled and boasted no large plantations or enslaved labor. Farmers barely eked out an existence. The 1860 U.S. Census showed about 3,500 residents in the county. Many Winstonians saw the impending conflict as "a rich man's war and a poor man's fight." They feared that the Civil War and the Confederacy were meant to maintain the political control of the wealthy planter class.

The election of Abraham Lincoln in 1860 wasn't seen as a threat to Winstonians, although most Winston County voters had supported Southern Democrat John C. Breckinridge for president. As a man of the people, Andrew Jackson was a hero to many Winston County residents, and Breckinridge was seen as Jackson's political heir. After all, many of these loyalists were descendants of Andrews Jackson's troops who had settled in the northern hills of Alabama. But Winston County inhabitants were also strongly Unionist. They supported Andrew Jackson, but they didn't support the Confederacy or slavery.

After Abraham Lincoln was elected, the Southern states began to secede from the Union. When Alabama called a convention to vote on the state seceding from the Union, Winston County chose twenty-two-year-old schoolteacher Christopher Sheats as its representative. Elected by an overwhelming majority on December 24, 1860, Sheats was an ardent Unionist. Sheats had vowed that, if elected to the convention, he would "vote against secession, first, last, and all of the time."

When Sheats refused to sign the secession ordinance at the Montgomery convention, he was expelled from the state legislature and imprisoned for a short time for treason. "I am an American," Sheats declared, "and an Alabamian. I don't need to sign anything to prove who I am."

Seeing their representative put in jail made the hill people of Winston County even angrier. Sheats was soon released from jail and sent home with a reminder to behave himself. If Alabama seceded from the Union, what options did Winston County have? A mass meeting at Looney's Tavern was called for July 4, 1861, to discuss the situation and to see what action Winston County should take.

To publicize the meeting, six men volunteered to ride in six different directions all over Winston County for six days to alert Winstonians. An estimated 2,500 people showed up. Three resolutions were presented and were overwhelmingly approved:

First: We commend the Hon. Chas. C. Sheats and the other representatives who stood with him for their loyalty and fidelity to the people whom they represented in voting against secession, first, last, and all of the time.

Second: We agree with Jackson that no state can legally get out of the union; but if we are mistaken in this, and a state can lawfully and legally secede or withdraw, being only a part of the Union, then a county, any county, being a part of the state, by the same process of reasoning, could cease to be a part of the state.

Third: We think that our neighbors in the South made a mistake when they bolted, resulting in the election of Mr. Lincoln, and that they made a greater mistake when they attempted to secede and set up a new government. However, we do not desire to see our neighbors in the South mistreated, and, therefore, we are not going to take up arms against them; but on the other hand, we are not going to shoot at the flag of our fathers, "Old Glory," the flag of Washington, Jefferson, and Jackson. Therefore, we ask that the Confederacy on the one hand, and the Union on the other, leave us alone, unmolested, that we may work out our political and financial destiny here in the hills and mountains of northwest Alabama.

When the gathering voted to be neutral in the Civil War, Confederate supporter Dick Payne blurted out, "Oh, oh, Winston secedes! The Free State of Winston."

Of course, Winston did not actually secede. But the county did go on to supply more troops for the Union than the Confederacy. And the nickname of "The Free State of Winston" still remains today.

During the Civil War, Winston County remained under state control and suffered violent acts of retribution during and after the war. In the first months after secession, many Unionists in Winston County formed home guard companies to defend themselves against Confederates. Many Winston supporters of the Confederacy volunteered for the Confederate Army at the beginning the war. On November 30, 1861, the county's Confederates held a meeting of their own and petitioned Governor John Gill Shorter to stifle the Union movement in the county, to require all county residents to take the Confederate loyalty oath, and to require the county to provide 250 Confederate soldiers.

Shorter's response was to issue writs of arrest for county residents who were actively disloyal to the Confederacy. He also demanded that militia commanders who would not take the oath of office should resign.

When Confederate conscription began in 1862, many Unionists fled their homes and hid in Winston County's rugged canyons and forests rather than fight with Confederate forces. Many of these men made their way north and joined the Union Army. With so many men gone from their farms, the county's residents had even more difficulty growing enough food to feed their families. That was made far worse when Confederate impressment agents took food and livestock from the county to feed the Confederate army.

Neighbor was pitted against neighbor in Winston County and both Unionists and Confederates engaged in vandalism, robbery, and even murder. One of the most notorious incidents involved probate judge Tom Pink Curtis, who was in charge of salt for distribution to the poor. Confederate horsemen captured Curtis in 1864 and took him to a bluff on Clear Creek where he was killed with two shots to his right eye.

Henry Tucker, a private in Company B of the First Alabama Cavalry was arrested by the Home Guard and tortured to death. Tucker's vicious death was then avenged when the Home Guard leader, Stoke Roberts, who had overseen Tucker's torture, was caught by a group of Unionists. Roberts was nailed to the root of a big oak tree by having a long iron spike driven into his mouth and out the back of his head.

After the war, considerable tension remained with occasional violence. Today, a statue of a Civil War soldier—half Union and half Confederate—stands in front of the Winston County Courthouse in Double Springs. The often-photographed statue commemorates the county's divided loyalties during the war.

ATTACK ON FORT MORGAN

1864

As the first light of dawn streaks the sky, a fleet of ships steams slowly toward the coast of Alabama. It is August 5, 1864, and the eighteen Union ships led by Admiral D. G. Farragut aim to get past Fort Morgan into Mobile Bay.

But Confederate defenders of the fort had other ideas.

At 7:30 a.m., as cannon fire reached a crescendo, the leading Union monitor, the *Tecumseh,* struck a mine—known as a torpedo during the Civil War. The *Tecumseh* sank within a minute, taking most of the crew with her. This sudden disaster threw the Union fleet into confusion, causing them to hesitate under the guns of Fort Morgan.

At this critical moment, Farragut gave his famous order, "Damn the torpedoes, full speed ahead!"

The rallying cry pushed the remaining vessels past the fort, through the minefield, and into Mobile Bay. The Confederates were soon forced to surrender.

And the rest is history.

Fort Morgan was one of the last Confederate forts to fall to Union forces. Twenty Confederate men were killed during the fall of the fort. About 500 were captured and sent to a Union prison in Elmira, New York. More than 140 of them died in that prison. Elmira had the highest death rate of any of the Union prisons—losing an average of 10 prisoners a day.

The Fort Morgan prisoners of war were particularly vulnerable in Elmira. These prisoners had been serving on the Gulf Coast of Alabama. They weren't acclimated to an upstate New York winter. Beset by pneumonia and unable to withstand the cold winter weather, Fort Morgan prisoners died in droves.

Now owned by the State of Alabama, the "Guardian of the Bay" is an interesting historical site with many stories to tell. Constructed with more than seven million bricks, Fort Morgan's star-shaped design provided protection for those soldiers keeping watch for enemy traffic into the port of Mobile

Construction on the fort began soon after the War of 1812 when Congress realized the need for stronger fortifications along the eastern and southern coastlines. When Fort Morgan was designed, Mobile was considered the backdoor to New Orleans. Part of the British plan during the War of 1812 was to take Mobile and use it as a base of operations against New Orleans.

Named for General Daniel Morgan, a Revolutionary War hero, the fort was completed in 1834 and first occupied in March of that year. The sally port or main entrance of the fort has the date "1833" over it, the year the fort was named, not the year it was completed.

But Fort Morgan and all her sister forts proved to be out of date during the Civil War. Rifled cannon and steam-powered warships repeatedly defeated the old brick forts. To strengthen the fort, concrete gun positions were added between 1896 and 1905 and were manned during the Spanish-American War and World War I. Because the fort was accessible primarily by water until after World War I, all supplies and building materials were brought to the site by ship.

Fort Morgan also was in use during World War II, but by that time the concrete batteries, like the brick fort before them, were no longer the primary defensive position. The fort was deactivated in 1923.

At one time, the fort had 100 wooden structures. All that remain are five: coast artillery's officers' quarters, staff officers' quarters, hospital stewards' quarters, the post bakery, and the post administration building. Flags fly over the site to show who once claimed the land: France, Great Britain, Spain, the United States, the Alabama Militia, the Confederacy, and the State of Alabama.

A museum chronicles the fort's importance from the War of 1812 through World War II. A variety of weapons, uniforms, and other artifacts tells the fort's story. The museum also offers a more personal look at fort life through the use of diaries, letters, and photographs from both the Union and the Confederate soldiers.

During the siege from August 5 to August 23, an officer at the fort wrote, "We are now in the hands of the Almighty and may He have mercy upon us."

A soldier from Iowa, who also had served as an artilleryman at Vicksburg, wrote that the bombardment at Fort Morgan was greater than what he suffered through at Vicksburg.

The fort also was the site of a freakish accident that took the life of Charles S. Stewart on April 30, 1863. Born in New York in 1828, Stewart moved to Alabama and became a successful merchant in Mobile and married Julia Brown. When Alabama seceded from the Union in 1861, Stewart cast his lot with his adopted state and joined the Mobile Cadets No. 2 of the Confederate army, proving to be a daring leader in the battles of Shiloh and Corinth.

Promoted to lieutenant colonel in May of 1862, Stewart was placed in command of Fort Morgan. He regularly wrote long letters home to his wife, some of which are displayed at the fort museum. Amid rumors of a powerful Union ironclad fleet preparing to attack Fort Morgan, Stewart decided to ready the fort, testing the fort's thirty-three pounder cannons.

On April 30, 1863, Stewart was standing by with other officers and his gun crew when one of the cannons was fired. Somehow by accident, the gun had been loaded with two powder charges instead of one. When the order to fire was given, the cannon exploded, spewing large pieces of metal.

Five soldiers were killed, including Stewart who died instantly when a 200-pound fragment struck him in the head. Years later, Stewart's granddaughter placed a marker on the steps of Fort Morgan, at the exact spot where Stewart was killed. Tradition says that stains from Stewart's blood are still visible on the steps.

At the beginning of the nineteenth century, another tragedy struck the area—the Great Hurricane of 1906. More than two hundred people were killed along the Gulf. The small village of Pilotstown, about three miles from the fort, was washed away by the hurricane and never rebuilt.

A sugar bowl now on display at the Fort Morgan museum was fished out of the bay about three years after the storm hit. Thrown out to sea when waters washed over a house, the sugar bowl was found with an oyster shell growing in it.

Only one soldier at the fort was killed during the hurricane. On guard duty during the middle of the hurricane, the soldier thought he heard someone calling for help on a pier. Thinking someone had fallen off the pier, the guard walked to the end of the pier with another man. As they got to the end of the pier, the pier collapsed. One man got away.

The guard was last seen clinging to the pier as it floated out to sea. There wasn't anything other soldiers could do but watch him die.

HELEN KELLER MEETS "THE MIRACLE WORKER"

1887

Three months before she turned seven years old, Helen Keller met the woman who would change her life forever. But the blind and deaf child wasn't at all happy about Anne Sullivan entering her home in Tuscumbia, Alabama, on March 3, 1887.

"Somehow I had expected to see a pale, delicate child. . . . But there's nothing pale or delicate about Helen," Sullivan wrote to a friend about that first meeting. "She is very quick tempered and willful, and nobody, except her brother James, has attempted to control her."

Helen wasn't always like this. She was born a healthy child on June 27, 1880, in a white frame cottage called Ivy Green. Her father, Captain Arthur Keller, was the editor of a local newspaper. Her mother was a beautiful woman named Kate Adams Keller.

Helen was a very active baby and began walking and talking early. Then when she was nineteen months old, Helen became very sick, diagnosed with brain fever, perhaps scarlet fever. The illness left her deaf and blind.

Unable to communicate, Helen became wild and uncontrollable, lost in utter silence and darkness. Her distraught parents were advised to place her in a home for the mentally retarded. Searching for alternatives, the Kellers contacted Dr. Alexander Graham Bell. A teacher of the deaf who had invented the telephone in 1876 partly in hopes that it might serve as a hearing aid, Bell suggested getting a teacher for Helen from the Perkins Institute.

That's how twenty-year-old Anne Sullivan came to arrive at the Keller home.

Sullivan knew firsthand how hellish life could be. Growing up in abject poverty, Sullivan suffered from a viral eye disease that left her half blind as a child. When her mother died and her father abandoned them, Annie and a brother were sent to the poor house for four years. She was saved when officials came to inspect reports of atrocities and the young girl flung herself at them, crying that she wanted to go to school.

When she was fourteen, Sullivan was transferred to the Perkins Institute and Massachusetts School for the Blind in Boston where her sight was partially restored and where she learned to spell and read Braille. Although her sight still was not clear, for the first time in her life, she could read.

Sullivan was the one chosen to share that world-opening ability with young Helen. But Helen was having no part of it. Their first meeting proved disastrous. When Helen's mother tried to control her, Helen began to clutch at her mother's dress and kick violently. That was only the beginning. Sullivan soon lost two teeth to Helen's violent tantrums.

Determined to exercise control and discipline over the child in order that she could learn, Sullivan asked that the two be sequestered away from Helen's indulgent parents in the Kellers' garden house. The spoiled child and her stubborn teacher had royal battles, but

Sullivan persevered in letting Helen know that she couldn't kick or hit people, that she couldn't eat off other's plates at meal times, and that she must act like a human being, not a wild animal. All the while, Sullivan spelled out words in the child's hand.

Helen quickly learned to form the letters correctly herself, but she did not know she was spelling a word or even that words existed. Helen stored up the spelling for many words without comprehending what they meant. When Sullivan handed her the doll that the children at Perkins had made for Helen and spelled "d-o-l-l" into the child's hand, Helen could repeat the action, but she didn't know what a doll was.

One day, Helen and teacher—as Helen always called Sullivan—went to the outdoor pump where Sullivan began pumping water. Putting the child's hand under the spout, Sullivan repeatedly spelled into the other hand the word "w-a-t-e-r."

"I stood still," Helen later wrote, "my whole body's attention fixed on the motions of her fingers as the cool stream flowed over my hand. All at once here was a strange stir within me—a misty consciousness, a sense of something remembered. It was as if I had come back to life after being dead!"

Eager to learn, Helen touched things one by one and asked their names. Sullivan told her. Helen mastered the alphabet, as well as Braille for blind readers. When she was nine years old, Helen decided she wanted to learn to speak with her voice. And she did. Although it was difficult for her to speak out loud clearly, Helen could talk.

When Helen was sixteen, she chose a new challenge. She wanted to go to a college where students could hear and see. She chose Radcliffe College in Massachusetts. Although Sullivan was almost always by her side signing class lectures into her hand, Helen wanted to be treated like the other students.

Helen earned excellent grades, and in one of her classes she wrote an essay about her life. When the essay came to the attention of the editor of *Ladies' Home Journal,* Helen was asked to write a series of articles about herself for the magazine. At age twenty-two, she published the articles in a book, *The Story of My Life.*

A year later, Helen graduated from Radcliffe with honors and continued to write. Since people were so curious about her, Helen Keller decided to give motivating lectures about her life and how others could overcome adversity. Keller also starred in a movie about her life called *Deliverance.*

In 1924, Keller became a member of a new organization called the American Foundation for the Blind. She toured the world, speaking about the struggles of the blind and raising money for the foundation.

On October 20, 1936, at age seventy, Anne Sullivan died. Her companion for almost fifty years, Helen Keller sat by her side and held her hand as she passed from life.

Keller continued to devote her life to others, traveling with her secretary, Polly Thomson. From 1943 to 1955, Helen traveled to military hospitals to visit wounded soldiers and encourage them to overcome their injuries. A film about her life, *The Unconquered* won an Academy Award in 1955. A 1962 movie, *The Miracle Worker,* gained Oscars for Anne Bancroft and Patty Duke for their portrayals of Anne Sullivan and Helen Keller.

When Thomson had a stroke and died March 21, 1960, her ashes were place next to Sullivan's. Winnie Corbally, who had taken care of Thomson, then became Keller's companion in her remaining years.

Over the years, Keller was honored with many awards and made friends with many world figures, among them John F. Kennedy, Charlie Chaplin, Mark Twain, William James, Nehru, Eleanor Roosevelt, Queen Elizabeth II of England, and Oliver Wendell Holmes.

After retiring from public life in 1961, Keller spent her days taking walks in her garden and reading books. She died of a heart attack on June 1, 1968, at eighty-seven years old. Thousands attended her funeral at the National Cathedral in Washington, D.C. Her ashes were placed in the cathedral next to those of her teacher and friend, Anne Sullivan.

Once asked if she believed in life after death, Helen Keller answered, "Most certainly. It is no more than passing from one room to another. . . . But there's a difference for me, you know. Because in that other room, I will be able to see."

GEORGE WASHINGTON CARVER ARRIVES AT TUSKEGEE INSTITUTE

1896

On a train ride to his new job at Tuskegee Institute in 1896, the professor looked out the passenger window and was dismayed at what he saw. On his journey through the South, he passed field after field of cotton crops and barren soil. Generations of hungry cotton had sucked nutrients out of the soil, draining it until it was depleted.

Reversing that waste would be his challenge, George Washington Carver decided. And that is exactly what he did.

Sounds like a mighty ambitious goal. But Carver had already overcome major obstacles that should have stopped him long ago. Born a slave, Carver was hit by deathly sickness, survived a kidnapping, and then was orphaned—all within the first year of his life.

In fact, Carver was never really sure when he was born. He always said it was near the end of the Civil War, probably around 1864. Born on a Missouri farm, young George was the son of two slaves. His father from a nearby farm died in a logging accident before George was born. Now no one even knows his name.

George's mother Mary was a slave on the 240-acre farm of Mary and Moses Carver in Diamond Grove, Missouri. She also had a daughter and a son, Jim, about five years older than George. One night when he was still a baby, George and his mother and sister were kidnapped by slave traders. Moses Carver hired someone to track down the thieves and bring back Mary and her babies. Left behind for dead because he was so sick with whooping cough, George was rescued and brought back to the farm. He never saw his mother or sister again.

"My body was very feeble, and it was a constant warfare between life and death to see who would gain the mastery," Carver later wrote.

The Carvers adopted the two orphans, who took Carver as their last name. A small sickly boy, George spent most of his time working around the house with his adopted mother, whom he called Aunt Sue. Older brother Jim worked in the fields alongside their adopted father, Uncle Moses. Later, Jim would die in adulthood of small pox.

When his chores were done, George loved to wander through the woods and meadows, marveling at the plants and animals. Wondering why some plants grew better than others, George started his own "secret" garden where he could tend and watch things grow. The boy experimented with soil, water, and sunshine. He also helped Aunt Sue tend her vegetable and flower gardens. The youngster became so skillful at caring for plants that neighbors nicknamed him "the Plant Doctor."

"Plants from all over the county would be brought to me for treatment," Carver wrote. "At this time I had never heard of botany and could scarcely read."

No one knew at the time how important that young boy and his plant experiments would become.

Thirsting for knowledge, George wanted to go to school, but the only schools near his home were for white children. When he was about twelve years old, George left home to attend an African-American school and stay with a black couple in nearby Neosho. To help earn his keep, he learned how to do laundry for his hosts. But, after about a year, George had exhausted his teacher's knowledge and was ready to move on to another school in another place, working odd jobs along the way. During his teenage years, George traveled across the Midwest searching for an education.

In order to avoid confusion with another George Carver, George gave himself a middle name—Washington. Carver lived in Minneapolis for about four years, attending school and running a successful laundry business. But he very much wanted to attend college and was so proud when he was accepted at Highland College in Kansas. He was devastated, however, when he showed up at Highland and was turned away because of his color. He never forgot the rejection and was surprised when Simpson College in nearby Indianola, Iowa, welcomed him as the only black student on campus.

To cover his tuition and living expenses, Carver taught guitar lessons, took in laundry, and did other odd jobs. Fellow students gave him furniture and sometimes slipped money and concert tickets under his door. An art major, Carver particularly enjoyed painting plants. Painting was a pastime he had picked up when he lived with the Carvers and saw his first paintings in the home of a neighbor. Since he didn't have paints, young George had made his own from plants and berries. For canvas, the boy painted on rocks, boards, and old cans. Painting was something he enjoyed for the rest of his life.

Although he was a talented artist, Carver was still fascinated by plants and what made them grow. To further his education, Carver transferred to nearby Iowa State College to study botany. He was almost thirty years old when he received his bachelor of agriculture from what is now Iowa State University, one of the first colleges in the nation to focus on farming research.

Taking odd jobs to make ends meet, Carver was also active in school organizations and continued his love of painting. One of his paintings was picked to represent Iowa at the World's Fair in Chicago in 1893. The first African American to attend the college, Carver couldn't sleep in the dorm or eat in the dining hall. He dined in the basement. But he endured and stayed to earn a master's degree in 1896.

Then he did something almost unheard of at the time—he became a college professor. As the only African American in the nation with advanced training in scientific agriculture, Carver was in demand at many colleges. But it was an Alabama college for black students that he chose.

Later called Tuskegee Institute and then Tuskegee University, the college was headed by Booker T. Washington. Since Carver was used to moving around, he expected to stay at Tuskegee for a few years. He ended up teaching there for the rest of his life.

When he first arrived at Tuskegee, Carver was shocked. His classroom was a shack, and his only real lab equipment was a microscope that his students and friends had given him as a going-away present from Iowa State. Carver had his work cut out for him in more ways than one. Students didn't want to be farmers. They saw how hard their parents worked on farms and how little money they made. The soil of the South was severely drained from continuous cotton plants. But Carver rolled up his sleeves and got to work.

He showed farmers how to rotate crops and build up the soil. Poor farmers couldn't afford expensive fertilizers. Carver showed them how to use manure and compost from decomposed grass, leaves, and other plant materials. He held farmers conferences, gave cooking demonstrations, organized agricultural fairs, published bulletins, and created a traveling wagon. Since some farmers couldn't come to Tuskegee, Carver took his education to them through his

Jessup Agricultural Wagon. Funded by a New Yorker named Morris K. Jessup, the horse-drawn wagon went on the road on May 24, 1906, to take Carver and his students out in the community to share seeds, plants, and advice.

In the early 1900s, boll weevils devastated the bolls—fluffy white parts—of the cotton plants. A curious thing Carver noted was that the weevils didn't touch peanut plants. The smart thing, Carver told farmers, was to grow peanuts. That was fine, but nobody seemed to want to buy the "goobers." Back then, peanuts were used mainly for hog food.

Since Carver had persuaded farmers to grow an abundance of peanuts, he thought he had better figure out more uses for the product. Locking himself in his lab, Carver experimented with ways that peanuts could be used. In only a couple of days, Carver had compiled an astonishing list of more than 300 uses for the amazing legume. In addition to tasty foods such as peanut butter, pancake flour, and candy, Carver listed numerous other peanut uses—anything from shampoo and shaving cream to gasoline and goiter medicine. He did similar research on soybeans, pecans, and sweet potatoes.

The famous "Peanut Man" was credited with helping save agriculture and the economy of the South. Honors and accolades poured his way. It was said that inventor Thomas Edison offered Carver a huge salary to work in his lab, but Carver chose to stay at Tuskegee and continue his research.

Sickened by pernicious anemia, Carver suffered a fall in December 1942 and died a few weeks later on January 5, 1943, at almost eighty years old. Although his salary never exceeded $1,500 a year, Carver donated his life savings to the George Washington Carver Foundation to help support agricultural research at Tuskegee. His savings added up to an astonishing $60,000.

BOOKS-A-MILLION STARTS AS HOMEMADE NEWSSTAND

1917

When his father died, fourteen-year-old Clyde W. Anderson dropped out of school to help support his family by delivering newspapers in 1917. Shortly thereafter, construction workers came to Anderson's hometown of Florence, Alabama, to build the new Wilson Dam.

When the boy heard workers saying how much they missed their hometown newspapers in the North, Anderson knew he had a new business. Gathering up old piano crates, Anderson fashioned a make-shift newsstand and contacted Northern newspaper publishers about sending their publications to Florence via the railroad.

Before long, Anderson had a booming business. Northern newspapers were delivered to his small newsstand and eagerly purchased by out-of-town workers. Within a few years, Anderson and his brother had enough profits saved to have a real bookshop in downtown Florence. And that was just the beginning.

In 1950, Clyde's son Charles C. Anderson inherited the bookstore and, it seems, some of his father's ambitious nature. Charles soon expanded the business into a chain of stores called Bookland. By 1980, Bookland had fifty stores located primarily in shopping malls around the Southeast. Charles also had established a book and periodical distribution business. When his sons—Charles Jr. and Clyde B.—were old enough, they also began working in the family business.

In the mid 1980s, Bookland bought Gateway Books, a chain of stores based in Knoxville, and doubled its size. However, this turned out not to be a good business move. Many Gateway stores weren't doing well and more than half of them were closed within two years. With so many stores out of business, the Anderson company had too many books and an excess of store fixtures on its hands.

The solution moved the Anderson family into a bigger and bolder business. In 1988, the youngest Anderson led the company to open an 8,000-square-foot store in a shopping center in Huntsville, Alabama. It was a flop. But it was also an important learning experience.

The next store that young Clyde B. Anderson opened was a superstore named Books-A-Million. Located down the street from the first one, the second store had 30,000 square feet as compared to the older one's 8,000. And the second store was successful as soon as it opened.

It was the right store for the right time. Superstores were the hit of the day. The formula quickly spread into other business concepts, allowing the stores to buy merchandise in bulk at cheaper prices and pass the savings along to customers. As even more enticement for shoppers, Books-A-Million sold bargain books at 40 to 90 percent of publisher's suggested retail prices. For high visibility, the sale books were placed prominently in front of the stores and updated weekly so that bargain hunters would want to keep coming back.

Another smart marketing technique was to allow individual Books-A-Million stores to offer a regional focus. For example, books about Alabama sports or high-profile Alabama personalities were given special publicity campaigns because those books often appealed to Alabama readers. Books-A-Million was also one of the first book superstores to open new stores in small cities instead of large metropolitan areas.

In 1992, the company changed its name to Books-A-Million, Inc., and went public on the NASDAQ exchange, selling 2.6 billion shares at $13 per share. Clyde B. Anderson became the chief executive officer. "Get to know your customers and give them what they want," Anderson told *Forbes* magazine, explaining the company's philosophy for success.

For example, when the University of Alabama upset Miami in the 1993 Super Bowl, the Anderson brothers knew that was big news. *Sports Illustrated* decided, however, that the story didn't rank being the magazine cover. So the Anderson brothers went to the magazine's editors and asked them to print 200,000 special editions of the publication with Alabama running back Derrick Lassic on the cover and more stories about the Alabama victory inside. Then Books-A-Million bought all 200,000 copies of the special commemorative issue.

Guess what! Books-A-Million was right on target. Within a month, the store had sold all the special Alabama issues, bringing in $900,000 and a neat estimated profit of $200,000.

By 1993, Books-A-Million had 113 stores in cities and small towns across the southeastern United States. The business also began offering extras such as coffee bars, free gift-wrapping, book searches for customers, and book signings. Encouraging children and families to read was a major focus of Books-A-Million with stores featuring separate Kids-A-Million departments, story hours, and videos for children.

"We're from a small town, and we wanted a concept that would work in a small town," Anderson said in a 1994 interview with

Retailing Today. "We found that some of these small towns couldn't support just a book store. But if you could have a combination book and something else—we developed a combination books and cards—that the economies of that may work."

In 1998, Books-A-Million launched its own website offering books at discounts. As an extra perk, Books-A-Million introduced its Joe Muggs Café with fireplaces, outdoor patios, more than 3,500 magazine titles, and a full line of specialty coffee drinks, tea, pastries, and other sweets.

Based in Birmingham, Books-A-Million is now the nation's third largest book retailer, behind Barnes & Noble and Borders. In its 2010 fiscal report, Books-A-Million noted that the company had 223 stores in twenty-two states and the District of Columbia with a net income of $13.8 million and about 5,500 full- and part-time employees. And it all started with a boy and his homemade news-stand in Alabama.

MONK BEGINS BUILDING MINIATURES

1918

As a Benedictine monk, Brother Joseph Zoettel didn't travel far beyond his monastery in Cullman, Alabama. But the man known as "Brother Joe" used his imagination to venture around the globe to exciting places whenever he wanted, and he left a legacy of travel beyond borders for others at his Alabama home.

Today, thanks to his artistic ability and patience, visitors can stroll past some of the world's greatest landmarks and can even see places that never really existed. Zoettel spent almost fifty years constructing more than 125 miniature reproductions of many of the world's most famous religious structures and landmarks. And he erected them right on the grounds where he spent most of his life.

A popular tourist destination, the Ave Maria Grotto is located in Cullman at Saint Bernard Abbey, Alabama's only Benedictine monastery. Spread over four lovely acres of the abbey's forested landscape, the creations are made of simple materials, much of it discarded until Zoettel visualized a new use for unwanted objects.

Born January 24, 1878, in Germany, Zoettel almost died at age thirteen when influenza swept Europe. When he was fourteen, Zoettel came to Saint Bernard as one of the first students of the newly founded college. It was a difficult decision for the young man to leave his family and homeland to journey to America to become a monk. It was also quite surprising for his parents.

"January 27, 1892, was the date of departure," Zoettel later wrote. "All night I cried till we entered the railroad car."

While studying for the priesthood, the young man was injured during a construction accident on campus and was left with a hunch-back for the rest of his life. But it didn't slow him down as a hard worker. His main job was among the most difficult at the monastery.

Put in charge of the powerhouse at the abbey, Zoettel spent thirty years working seventeen-hour days, even on Sunday, to keep the powerhouses running on coal. "It became very tedious for I had to pump from morning to night every day. . . . To pass the time, I started hobbies again."

First, he made small grottoes, which were sold to visitors to support the abbey's work. Starting in 1918, Zoettel began crafting models with materials left over from construction of the monastery's buildings.

"One day Father Dominic came to me with some little statues and to see if I could make small grottoes," Zoettel later said. "He had a store in front of the college and sold religious articles to help missions. When I had made two grottoes, I thought that would be all, but as Father Dominic sold them right way, he always brought more statues, and it became a regular business."

Before long, Zoettel had made five thousand small grottoes for sale. Then he turned his attention to larger projects.

Most of his creations are models of Christian sites around the world: Lourdes Cathedral in France, the World Peace Church in

Hiroshima, the Vatican's St. Peter's Basilica, and many more. He even crafted a miniature Saint Bernard's Abbey, complete with the abbey's power station where he worked shoveling coal.

Tiny replicas include the Leaning Tower of Pisa, Grotto of St. Theresa, Hanging Gardens of Babylon, Our Lady of Guadalupe Shrine, Great Wall of China, and tiny versions of Jerusalem, Bethlehem, and Rome. One half of the hillside features buildings and scenes from the Holy Land.

Zoettel also paid homage to his new homeland by creating the Statue of Liberty and the Alamo. The craftsman showed his whimsy with such junk-bejeweled fantasies as Hansel and Gretel Visit the Temple of the Fairies and The Tower of Thanks.

Since he hadn't seen many of the real buildings in person, Zoettel used photographs and postcards for his replicas. That's why many of the replicas are tucked into hillside settings. Zoettel didn't really know what was on the backs and sides of things since he never saw them in person. The scale isn't accurate, of course. Some of the towers and buttresses are a bit too large or too small, but they are as the artist envisioned them.

At first Zoettel's works were enjoyed only by fellow monks. The original dozen or so sculptures were located in an abbey garden closed to the public. Then people began to hear about the unusual collection and wanted to see it, too.

"By and by other people came, and it became a real nuisance which could not be stopped anymore," Zoettel wrote. Because of public interest, the monks decided to move Zoettel's work to a special place, a grotto on the site of a quarry near the monastery where visitors could see the displayed models without disturbing the monks' prayerful life.

After two years, the Ave Maria Grotto was completed. In 1934, the monks moved the replicas to their present site and opened it to the public. The centerpiece of the park is the Ave Maria Grotto itself, which was dedicated in 1934 and by which the whole collection is now known. In 1984, the collection was listed on the National Registry of Historic Places.

Dedicated to the Virgin Mary, the grotto, or cave, features a life-size statue set in a space twenty-seven feet high, twenty-seven feet wide and twenty-seven feet deep. The manmade cave is filled with glittering stalactites of colored glass, stones, and shells. Part of that glitter came from an unexpected source when an L&N train car derailed about twenty miles away on April 28, 1933. Zoettel had been considering what special material he could use for his grotto when the solution was presented to him.

One freight car filled with marble from the Gantt Quarry in Sylacauga overturned, and the marble was crushed. Since the owner could no longer use the broken marble, he gave it to Saint Bernard. The monks carted it to their brother who used it to produce the main stalactites hanging in the Great Grotto. Zoettel then embellished his grotto with seashells, colored stone, tiles, and glass.

Other materials also came from donations from people who had seen and admired Zoettel's projects. No matter what it was, the talented monk seemed to find just the right place for it. From every state and many foreign countries, the trinkets and treasures poured in—cold cream jars, plastic animals, costume jewelry, broken bathroom tile, marbles, colored glass, and even toilet seats.

Building each structure from cement, marble, and wood, Zoettel then would visualize how to use the gifts at hand. For his personal Tower of Thanks, the artist used four green glass balls, each one set atop a four-foot spire. The balls came from Ireland and were originally used as floats for fishing nets.

On the fantasy side, a dragon is made of bits of stone, marbles, and green tile. Plastic toy elephants romp around replicas of the

Great Pyramid and the Hanging Gardens of Babylon. A rusty bird-cage became the base for a replica of St. Peter's Cathedral dome. For his tiny columns, Zoettel filled small glass apothecary tubes with cement. When the cement had dried, he broke the glass and had perfect mini columns. Old toilet bowl floats became domes and pieces of broken colored glass were fashioned into small stained-glass windows.

Zoettel continued to work until 1958, when at the age of eighty, he built his last model, the basilica in Lourdes. He died three years later on October 15, 1961, and is buried in a special bronze coffin in the abbey cemetery.

BOLL WEEVIL MONUMENT

1919

Standing smack dab in the middle of a busy intersection in downtown Enterprise, Alabama, is a statue of a lovely lady. But wait, there's more. The "more" is what causes motorists and pedestrians alike to do a double take. Over her head, the sculptured woman triumphantly holds a large insect. The multi-legged critter is a boll weevil.

The scourge of the South, the boll weevil was a major agricultural pest that devoured huge fields of cotton crops. So why erect a statue to such a destructive beetle? Because the boll weevil and its ravenous appetite for cotton forced Alabama farmers to diversify, leading them to plant successful new crops, particularly peanuts.

"In profound appreciation of the boll weevil and what it has done as the herald of prosperity," reads the inscription on the monument. Placed on the site on December 11, 1919, the memorial has drawn much attention, vandalism, and even some jokes. But the reasons for its being are quite serious.

Back in the 1890s, the boll weevil expanded from Mexico into the United States. It quickly ate its way across the cotton fields of the South and arrived in Alabama sometime in the 1910s. Known as *Anthonomus grandis,* the boll weevil is a small, grayish-brown beetle about one-fourth of an inch long. Using a long, sharp beak or snout, the female pierces cotton flower buds and then deposits within each bud an egg that hatches into a larva. The larva feeds on the inside of the bud, causing it to wilt and drop off the stem. The larva develops into a beetle that continues to feed on the buds and bolls, the unopened seedpods.

Since Alabama's economy was based almost entirely on agriculture, the arrival of the boll weevil scourge was ruinous. With cotton being the primary cash crop, farmers and the many industries that depended on them were devastated. Boll weevils had infested the entire state by 1916 with losses of 60 to 75 percent of the cotton crops. Economic losses to the weevil in Alabama were $20 million to $40 million each year for more than eighty years.

In the early years of the infestation, farmers tried many methods of eradication. They used homemade insecticides and controlled burning to try and kill the weevils or minimize the insect damage. They tried planting earlier, hoping to harvest the cotton before the bugs could get at it. Nothing worked in the long-term.

At the urging of Extension Service agents, farmers began using the insecticide calcium arsenate in 1918. That provided relief for a while. Then scientists developed a new class of insecticides, including DDT. These chlorinated hydrocarbons were very effective—until the weevil developed a resistance to the chemicals. Also the insecticides remained in the soil and water and were harmful to birds, fish, and other wildlife.

In the early 1960s, scientists created an even more effective class of chemical insecticide, which did not linger in the environment. But the new chemicals were extremely toxic to humans and other warm-blooded animals. In fact, the new chemistry began with the development of toxic nerve gases used during World War II.

In 1979, the U.S. Department of Agriculture set up a large-scale program for eradication that included pheromone traps. Baited with a synthetic weevil mating attractant, the traps would detect where weevils still existed. Then Malathion would be sprayed on infested fields, sometimes as often as twenty sprays a year for several years.

Since 1995, no economic damage resulting from the weevil has been reported from Alabama. The last weevil captured was a single find in Mobile County in 2003.

But the blasted bug turned out to be a blessing in disguise. With cotton crops being eaten right before their eyes, farmers turned to planting other crops, such as peanuts, which could be grown on the same land and bring new money to the area. Taking the advice of such agricultural scientists as Tuskegee Institute's George Washington Carver, farmers planted peanuts, sweet potatoes, corn, and soybeans.

The story goes that local businessman H. M. Sessions could see the writing on the wall when the weevil hit town. He was convinced that planting peanuts was the answer. In 1916, he convinced deeply indebted farmer C. W. Bastion to give peanuts a chance for one year. To sweeten the offer, Sessions tossed in the peanuts for planting, a picker to harvest them, and a price of $1 a bushel.

The gamble paid off. Bastion harvested eight thousand bushels of peanuts. Other farmers used some of the peanuts as seed to get into the peanut-growing business themselves. Coffee County rebounded economically in 1917 with the largest peanut harvest in the nation. King Cotton no longer reigned over Alabama.

More modern agricultural practices also were developed because of the boll weevil epidemic, and the Cooperative Extension Service was created. Although cotton has once again become a viable agricultural crop in southern Alabama, it is still rotated with peanut crops, which is better for the soil and for the economy.

In 1919, Enterprise city councilman Roscoe Owen "Bon" Fleming suggested honoring the insect that turned around Enterprise's economy. The memorial also would salute those fine folks who had adjusted and thrived in the face of adversity.

Built in Italy for about $1,800, the statue consisted of a life-sized Classical Greek female figure in a flowing gown standing atop a pedestal. Surrounded by a fountain, the woman held a small fountain above her head in her outstretched arms. The stone monument was dedicated on December 11, 1919, at the intersection of College and Main Streets, the heart of the town's business district.

About thirty years later, artist Luther Baker reckoned that the statue was lacking something very important—a boll weevil. So Baker fashioned a four-legged model of the insect from linotype metal. The small fountain was removed and the boll weevil was mounted atop the lady's outstretched arms. That lasted about four years until the boll weevil was stolen in 1953. It was replaced with a larger, more accurate sculpture with six legs.

Both the lady and her bug have had some interesting adventures over the years. Pranksters have poured detergents and soaps in the fountain so it would bubble over. Baby alligators and other foreign objects have showed up in the fountain. In the 1970s, both the boll weevil and the lady disappeared and were found two days later alongside a road. Local metal fabrications repaired the damaged monument.

In 1981, the insect was stolen again and replaced with a new version. But the most damaging incident happened on July 11, 1998, when vandals tore the boll weevil out of the statue's upstretched hands, ripping part of her arms and tearing cracks down her back. After an anonymous tip, two local boys were arrested and led police to where the weevil was buried in a wooded area near the country club. But the bug was damaged so severely that it couldn't be easily plunked back on top, and the lady was in dire need of repairs.

After five months of emptiness, a replica was erected on the monument base. The sturdier copy had been made from a mold used to create a life-size double that had been displayed in the Atlanta History Museum from summer 1996 until fall 1997. Before the city's annual Christmas parade on December 15, 1998, thousands of spectators cheered while red, white, and blue balloons were released to welcome back the town's symbol.

City leaders initially intended to repair the original monument and put it back in its downtown spot. However, the project proved too costly. Instead, the copy still stands in downtown Enterprise and the original is safely on display less than a block away at the Enterprise Depot Museum. A security camera now guards the outside monument which is surrounded by a spear-tipped fence to prevent further shenanigans.

The statue caper did bring some national and international attention to the town, including one "news" report that many citizens would rather forget. *The Daily Show* on Comedy Central latched onto the story and aired a segment on August 13, 1998. *Daily Show* correspondent and comedian A. Whitney Brown reported on the segment that, "For generations, inhabitants have worshipped the boll weevil with a pagan fervor around a sacred idol to the insect pest in the town square. And all was well in Boll Weevil City until someone stole their magic weevil."

The premise of the show joked that the residents of Enterprise worshipped the weevil and that the city had fallen on hard times when the idol was displaced. To make it even worse—or humorously realistic, depending on the watcher's point of view—the show interviewed several of the city's prominent citizens who thought they were taking part in an actual NBC news show. Suffice it to say, the interviewees were shocked to find out they were being poked fun at by a mock news show. But, as they had before, the enterprising folks of Enterprise survived the latest invasion by a different media pest.

THE POET OF TOLSTOY PARK

1925

When a doctor told Henry Stuart that he only had a year to live, the Idaho man decided to leave town. Diagnosed with consumption, the sixty-seven year old figured he might as well die in the little place known as Fairhope, Alabama.

Stuart didn't know a soul there, but he must have thought that the community founded in 1894 by utopian dreamers would be a good place to face his imminent demise. The waterside town on the eastern shore of Mobile Bay has long been a refuge for independent thinkers and proudly eccentric characters.

Acquiring about ten acres, Stuart built a small round hurricane-proof hut out of concrete. Making all the concrete bricks himself, Stuart dated each one, maybe as a reminder that he had been there.

An admirer of famed author Tolstoy, Stuart named his patch of ground Tolstoy Park. It took him a year and sixteen days in 1925 and 1926 to construct the hut all by himself. Shaped somewhat like a beehive, the diameter of the floor, fourteen feet, perfectly matched the distance between the floor and the top of the hut's domed roof.

The hut was also dug sixteen inches into the ground, which at that depth is a constant fifty-seven degrees, making the floor cool in the summer and warm in the winter.

For his bed, Stuart had a hammock that swayed twenty feet off the ground. The only way to get into bed was by climbing up a ladder. Stuart also kept a loom that he used to weave rugs, which he sold for a living.

Stuart decided he wasn't going to wear shoes, but he found out that he needed one shoe at least. He had to have a shoe on his foot to push down hard enough on a shovel. He went to a store and tried to buy one shoe for his right foot. When they said they couldn't sell just one shoe, Stuart bought the pair and told them to keep the left shoe for someone who needed it. Old photographs show Stuart going barefoot, even in the depths of winter.

Although he was known as the Hermit of Montrose (a neighborhood in Fairhope), Stuart seemed to have plenty of visitors. More than 1,200 people signed a guest book he kept in his hut, including Clarence Darrow, the noted Chicago lawyer of Scopes Monkey Trial fame.

Of course, the shoeless man with the long white beard did die. But it was long after his Idaho doctor had told him he would. Stuart died in 1946 at eighty-eight years of age.

His hut still stands, now surrounded by office buildings. It rests just off the parking lot of a real estate office. And thanks to the writings of a local man, the tale of Henry Stuart and his unusual home is now enjoying a resurgence with people around the world.

Sonny Brewer discovered Henry Stuart's hut in the 1980s when he was driving through Fairhope on his way to a real estate seminar. Brewer saw the crazy little house and wanted to know more about the unusual fella who built it. Researching old newspaper articles and photos, Brewer became intrigued by Stuart's story.

Although he started out to write a nonfiction account of Stuart's life, Brewer changed his mind and settled on fiction instead because he didn't want to have to deal with total accuracy in his tale telling.

Quitting his real estate job, Brewer opened an independent bookstore called Over the Transom in Fairhope. Trying to sell an autobiography novel about his own life to pay the bills, Brewer was about at the end of his financial rope. The novel about his life wasn't selling, and his bookstore was losing money big time. Brewer's literary agent asked if he had anything else to submit. Remembering his fascination with Stuart, Brewer submitted the first twenty pages of a story on *The Poet of Tolstoy Park,* along with a six-page outline. Ballantine bought the novel for $100,000.

Then Brewer was faced with the deadline of actually writing the novel. For inspiration, Brewer convinced the local banker who owned the land with the hut to rent it to him for $9 a month. Cleaning out debris, replacing windows, and removing a wooden floor, Brewer moved in to add the finishing touches to his book—writing it the way he thought Stuart might like—barefoot.

When he was finished, Brewer placed a copy of his manuscript in the hut and left the door unlocked. Somewhere along the line, people began making pilgrimages to Stuart's old home, often leaving money in an iron skillet in the hut. Stuart was well-known to be generous with loans, never asking for repayment. The money that suddenly appeared in the hut seemed to be a legacy of Stuart's generosity—sometimes some of the money would disappear, other times even more would be left in the pile.

Brewer's book, *The Poet of Tolstoy Park,* was published in 2006. The novel sold out its first printing in forty-eight hours and was selected by the Book of the Month Club and One Spirit Book Club. A movie deal based on the book has been signed, and Brewer hopes to get the hut placed on the National Register of Historic Places to help preserve it in perpetuity.

THE SCOTTSBORO BOYS

1931

Hoping to find work during the Great Depression, nine young black men hopped a freight train. Riding the rails as hobos was a common practice during this bleak period of economic turmoil, but this particular train ride would change the lives of the teens who came to be called the "Scottsboro Boys." The tragedy split the nation and dragged on for almost half a century. In truth, the saga still continues.

It started on March 25, 1931, shortly after the train passed into Alabama when a fight broke out between some white boys and some of the black hobos. The story goes that a white freight hopper walked across the top of a tank car shortly after the train rumbled into Alabama and stepped on the hand of one of the blacks, Haywood Patterson, who was hanging onto the train's side. A stone-throwing, name-calling, fist-flying fight ensued between the two groups, with the blacks forcing the whites off the train at the next stop.

Angry, the white group told the stationmaster that they had been assaulted by a gang of blacks. The stationmaster wired ahead to the next stop to have the black youths apprehended. When the train stopped just outside of Paint Rock, local police, along with a gun-toting mob, rounded up nine African Americans ranging in age from thirteen to nineteen. The boys were roped together, loaded onto a flatbed truck, and hauled off to jail, where they were charged with assault.

Later, two young white women from Huntsville also were found hitching a ride on the same train. Allegedly a known prostitute, Victoria Price (age nineteen) was facing vagrancy and morality charges, possibly violating the Mann Act, which prohibited taking a minor across state lines for prostitution. Ruby Bates was underage at seventeen. Upon questioning by police, the two women said they had been raped by the young black men. A local doctor and his assistant examined the women and reported no evidence of a violent attack although semen was present in both. The two women were never charged and were released.

The accused—Olen Montgomery (age seventeen), Clarence Norris (age nineteen), Haywood Patterson (age eighteen), Ozzie Powell (age sixteen), Willie Roberson (age sixteen), Charlie Weems (age sixteen), Eugene Williams (age thirteen), and brothers Andy Wright (age nineteen) and Roy Wright (age thirteen)—were arrested and taken to the Jackson County seat of Scottsboro to await trial.

What happened next is said to have been a major catalyst for the modern civil rights movement. The case also was also said to have provided inspiration for Alabama writer Harper Lee's Pulitzer Prize–winning novel *To Kill a Mockingbird*.

The assigned defense attorney was known as an incompetent town drunk. He spent just twenty-five minutes with the defendants before the trials started. Trials took only four days in early April. The accused were tried in four groups while angry white mobs gathered outside the courthouse. Afraid of a lynching, Governor Benjamin Miller sent the Alabama National Guard to Scottsboro to keep the peace.

Not surprisingly, each of the four all-white male juries returned guilty verdicts in just a matter of hours. Eight defendants were sentenced to death. The youngest defendant—thirteen-year-old Roy Wright—got a split jury, half wanting death and the other half wanting life imprisonment for the boy. The judge ruled a mistrial, and Wright was held in prison for the next six years awaiting a new trial. The other eight men were sentenced to be executed on July 10, the earliest date possible under the law.

The case might have ended there with the world never knowing what had happened. But a radical legal action organization known as the International Labor Defense stepped in. Sponsored by the Communist Party USA, the ILD saw the case as a powerful propaganda tool and a way to recruit members to the Communist Party. The ILD also knew that storm clouds were gathering for a national struggle against racism, and this case might be the match needed to light the fight.

Through ILD promotional efforts, people around the nation heard of the Scottsboro Nine case, and the ILD secured a stay of execution until the case could be heard by the Alabama Supreme Court. At the same time, the National Association for the Advancement of Colored People was slowly stepping up to the fray, although the NAACP had initially avoided involvement.

To get its message across, the ILD organized rallies, parades, speaking tours, and a media blitz that proclaimed the flaws in a legal system that would railroad defendants such as the Scottsboro Nine. Suddenly, the local case had the gaze of the world turned upon it and upon Alabama. Protests against the verdicts and the legal system took place around the globe.

The Alabama Supreme Court heard the ILD appeal but upheld the convictions. In November 1932, the ILD turned to the U.S. Supreme Court and got the convictions overturned and new trials ordered for all the defendants. Labeled *Powell v. Alabama,* the Supreme Court's ruling established an important precedent for enforcing African Americans' right to adequate counsel under the equal protection clause of the Fourteenth Amendment.

Despite overwhelming evidence of their innocence, the Scottsboro defendants remained imprisoned. One of the accusers herself, Ruby Bates, recanted her story and said she had made up the rape claims. She even agreed to testify for the defense, as did a doctor who had examined Bates and Price on the day of the alleged rape and said that he saw no signs of rape. In December 1933, Haywood Patterson and Clarence Norris were convicted of rape and sentenced to death for a third time by another all-white male jury. Awaiting new trials, the five other defendants stayed in prison while the remaining two were sent to juvenile court and later convicted.

In April of 1935, the U.S. Supreme Court once again overturned the guilty verdicts of Patterson and Norris and ordered new trials, ruling that the defendants were denied a fair trial because African Americans were excluded from Jackson County jury rolls. That landmark decision led to the integration of juries across the nation.

In January 1936, Patterson was convicted of rape for a fourth time and sentenced to seventy-five years in prison. The verdict represented the first time in the history of Alabama that a black man convicted of raping a white woman had not been sentenced to death. In an apparent escape attempt, Ozzie Powell was shot in the head after attacking a deputy sheriff. Powell survived but suffered permanent brain damage. To end the long legal ordeal, the Scottsboro Defense Committee and the prosecution agreed to a weird deal. On the basis of the very same evidence, four defendants were set free and four were convicted.

Clarence Norris was convicted of rape and sentenced to death, which was commuted to life imprisonment by Alabama governor

Bibb Graves. Andy Wright and Charlie Weems also were convicted of rape and sentenced to lengthy prison terms. Powell was convicted of assaulting the deputy sheriff and sentenced to twenty years, but his rape charges were dropped. All charges were dropped against Roy Wright, Olen Montgomery, Willie Roberson, and Eugene Williams.

A final attempt to free the four convicted failed in 1938 when pardon applications were denied by the Alabama Pardon Board and by Governor Graves. Charlie Weems was paroled in 1943. Clarence Norris and Andy Wright were paroled in 1944, but sent back to prison shortly afterward for violating terms of their probation by leaving the state.

Ozzie Powell was paroled in 1946. Haywood Patterson escaped from prison in 1948. Norris—the last surviving "Scottsboro Boy"—was pardoned in 1976, almost half a century after the crime for which he and the others claimed innocence. Norris died in 1989.

The Scottsboro Boys legacy, however, lives on. Books have been written, documentaries and movies made, blues singer Leadbelly recorded a song "Scottsboro Boys," and in 2010 a musical about the tragedy opened on Broadway.

Written by theater giants John Kander and Fred Ebb, who partnered for the legendary musicals *Chicago* and *Cabaret*, *The Scottsboro Boys* came to the stage.

COON DOG GRAVEYARD

1937

A small grassy meadow marks the final resting place of faithful coon dog Troop. Key Underwood and his canine buddy had romped together through these woods, spending many happy days and nights doing what they loved.

After hunting together for more than fifteen years, Troop died on the day before Labor Day in 1937. It was only fitting, Underwood decided, that his close friend should spend eternity at the old campsite in Northwest Alabama where he had been most happy.

Wrapping Troop in a cotton sack, Underwood gave him a fitting funeral on a dreary Labor Day. Digging a hole three feet under, Underwood solemnly said farewell to his friend. Choosing a rock from a nearby old chimney, Underwood used a hammer and screwdriver to chisel out Troop's name and date. The stone was erected over the grave as a special marker for what many considered to be the best coon dog in the area.

Half redbone coonhound and half birdsong, Troop was an expert at finding his prey. He was "cold nosed," meaning he could follow cold raccoon tracks until they grew fresh. It was said that Troop never left the trail until he had treed the coon.

That might have been the end of it.

However, several years later, Underwood's brother lost one of his beloved coon dogs and decided to lay his dog to rest near Troop. Then the two brothers figured they needed to protect the spot known as Sugar Creek about seven miles west of Tuscumbia. Leasing the site from a lumber company that owned the land at the time, the brothers named the spot the Key Underwood Coon Dog Memorial Graveyard. Little did they know the tradition they were starting more than seven decades ago.

Now the cemetery is home to more than 220 coon dog graves and hosts a celebration each Labor Day. Even on ordinary days, visitors check with the local Colbert County Tourist and Convention Bureau for a brochure and directions to the cemetery. The graveyard is open every day from dawn to dusk. Located in the wilderness off Freedom Hills, the cemetery is the only one of its kind in the world.

In order to be buried here, a coonhound must meet three requirements:

1. The owner must claim their pet is an authentic coon dog.
2. A witness must declare the deceased as a coon dog.
3. A member of the local coon hunters organization must be allowed to view the coon dog and declare it as such.

Although a pedigree or special breed is not required for qualification, the dog must have been a hunting dog and must have hunted raccoons exclusively. Many famous dogs are now honored with burials at the cemetery, such as Hunter's Famous Amos, Ralston Purina's 1984 Dog of the Year.

A granite monument marks the entrance to the Key Underwood Coon Dog Memorial Graveyard, established September 4, 1937.

The eye-catching memorial shows two dogs barking up a tree. Made of wood, granite, metal, and natural stone, grave markers range from simple homemade ones to more elaborate professionally engraved stones such as those found at human cemeteries. The stones feature names of the much-missed dogs: Hatton's Blue Flash, High Pocket, Patches, Preacher, Night Ranger, Bean Blossom Bomma, Smoky, Daisy, Black Ranger, Bear, Easy Going Sam, Bragg, Gypsy, Old Tip, Doc, Old Roy, and more.

Many of the stones have rusting dog collars looped over them and heartfelt sentiments such as "The best east of the Mississippi," "Ability and class in one," "As good as the best," "A joy to hunt with," "He wasn't the best, but he was the best I ever had," and the simple message "My best friend."

Fresh flowers and artificial ones often decorate the graves. Some of the stones bear the breed of the dog and the owner's name. Several championships dogs are buried in the cemetery, which averages about three burials a year.

"When I buried Troop, I had no intention of establishing a coon dog cemetery," Underwood said. "I merely wanted to do something special for a special coon dog."

When Labor Day rolls around, the Tennessee Valley Coon Hunters Association holds a celebration at the cemetery. After cleaning and decorating the graves, the group and guests enjoy music, a barbecue, and a liar's contest at the public gathering. Many of the tall tales stretch the truth about the supreme hunting expedition or the most amazing coon dog exploits.

Legend says that on the night of Labor Day, if you listen closely you can hear the ghost of old Troop running through the woods and howling as he hunts beneath the moon.

TUSKEGEE AIRMEN

1941

When First Lady Eleanor Roosevelt arrived at Tuskegee on April 19, 1941, folks were honored to have the president's wife visiting. But people were not prepared for what Eleanor Roosevelt did next.

Climbing in a two-seater plane, Roosevelt and pilot Charles Anderson took off into the wild blue yonder. Officials were speechless with fear. Secret Service agents were aghast. Some wanted to call the president and get him to stop her. After a thirty-minute flight, the plane safely glided back into the airport.

"Well, he can fly alright!" the first lady announced to the waiting crowd and the media.

Not only did Roosevelt surprise the nation with her unexpected flight, she also let everyone know that she trusted her life to the skill of an African-American pilot. That was an important step in providing the funding and support needed to build a field to train the Tuskegee Airmen.

A photo snapped of Roosevelt in the plane with Anderson in the cockpit hit newspapers around the country. "That plane ride did more for black aviation than anything had before," Anderson later said.

Back then, racial discrimination was rampant, and many people believed that African Americans did not have the brains or the courage or the patriotism to be pilots. From the beginning of the U.S. Army Air Service in 1907, African Americans were not admitted to flying programs.

When President Franklin Delano Roosevelt took office, he began looking for ways to provide more military protection for the nation in the event of the inevitable war that loomed on the horizon. Civilian pilots seemed a viable option. The Civilian Pilot Training Program of the Civil Aeronautics Authority authorized the flight training of twenty thousand college students per year. The idea was that these civilian pilots could be adapted to military flying in case war broke out and the nation needed to expand its air support very quickly.

As part of that reasoning, an "experiment" was proposed in December 1940 by the Army Air Corps to establish an all-black fighter squadron. African-American leaders had been urging the use of black fighter pilots for quite some time. Blacks had already proven for years that they could fly. One African-American pilot, Eugene Jacques Bullard, had flown with the French Air Force in World War I from 1914 to 1918. He was widely regarded as a hero.

Next the government had to decide on the location of a field to train those black pilots. To the consternation of many, the choice was the Deep South in Tuskegee. Alabama in 1940 was a stronghold of racial intolerance and the experiment seemed doomed from the start. A strong reason for the selection of Tuskegee was that it was already the home of a famous black institution that stood for self-help and self-determination. Tuskegee Institute was built by Booker T. Washington, the former slave who had become one of the nation's most prominent and respected leaders before his death in 1915.

So Tuskegee it was. On July 19, 1941, the Tuskegee Army Air Field officially opened, and the first members of the 99th Pursuit Squadron arrived for combat flight training.

Thirteen started in the initial class. Coming to the Deep South from the North, the African-American trainees had to learn to live under Jim Crow laws. Everything was separate and enforced by law.

The first black trainees ate in separate mess halls, used separate bathrooms, and played at separate recreation facilities. No black officers belonged to the officers' club. Off base, the situation was even worse. There were few places for a black person to eat, shop, or enjoy recreation or entertainment. There were no local hotels that accepted blacks. Schools were segregated.

Since the rigidly segregated unit required a black leader, Captain Benjamin O. Davis, a West Point Academy graduate, was picked to head the outfit. After all, he was one of only two black officers in the army—the other was his father.

Although it seemed designed to fail, the experimental program was successful against all odds. Led by Davis, Tuskegee's first group of five men graduated on March 7, 1942. When called into action in World War II, the Tuskegee Airmen, as they were nicknamed, became known for their courage, dedication, and exceptional skill as pilots.

While the Tuskegee airmen were still in training, the nation had united in horror when Japanese forces attacked the U. S. Naval Base at Pearl Harbor on December 7, 1941. The next day, the United States had entered World War II against Germany, Italy, and Japan.

Three months after America entered the war, four cadets and their captain graduated from pilot training at Tuskegee and made history. They were the first African Americans to receive their pilot wings. By the end of the 1942, the 99th Fighter Squadron was ready to enter the war in Europe. But the Tuskegee Airmen were told they needed even more training, more than was required of white cadets. On April 15, 1943, the outfit was finally shipped out to North Africa and stationed in Tunisia.

Eager to show what they could do, the Tuskegee Airmen didn't have to wait long. On June 2, 1943, the 99th Fighter Squadron launched its first ground-strafing attack. Flying at low altitude, the squadron fired machine guns at targets on the ground such as bridges and truck convoys. The pilots also dropped bombs on targets identified by intelligence officers. The squadron scored its first victory by shooting down a German fighter plane. That same day, the group also suffered its first loss when two 99th Squadron pilots collided their planes that morning, killing both men.

During the summer and fall of 1943, the Tuskegee Airmen worked mainly as support operations, carrying out strafing missions of ammunition dumps, supply routes, tanks, trucks, and trains. The squadron seldom encountered enemy aircraft. That changed when the Tuskegee Airmen were transferred in October 1943 to the 79th Fighter Group. Now they flew in formation with white pilots and were regarded as equals.

During the three-day battle over Anzio, Italy, in January 1944, Tuskegee Airmen downed seventeen German planes. "And that was the turning point of the history and the fortunes of the 99th," said pilot Lemuel Rodney Curtis.

In June 1944, the Tuskegee Airmen got another important assignment as fighter escorts to the 332nd Fighter Group. The Airmen's job was to protect bombers seeking to destroy German weapons and supplies. In their first forty days, the 332nd shot down forty enemy planes without losing a single bomber to enemy fighters. The Tuskegee Airmen were soon regarded as tops at their job. No bomber escorted by the Tuskegee Airmen was ever shot down or abandoned in the heat of battle.

"There's no such thing as segregation when you're fighting side by side," Tuskegee Airman Wilson V. Eagleson said.

When the Tuskegee Airmen were assigned to fly the air force's newest fighter, the P-51 Mustangs, they painted the tails of their planes bright red, earning them the nickname the "Red-Tailed Angels."

"It was a wondrous sight to see those escort fighter planes coming up to take care of us, escorting us into the targets, picking us up after the bombing raids and taking us home," said bomber pilot George McGovern, who later served as a senator and ran for president. "They were flown by men with enormous skill and coordination."

By the spring of 1945, the Tuskegee Airmen had downed 111 enemy aircraft and destroyed another 150 on the ground. They sank one German destroyer and forty other boats and barges. They disabled more than six hundred ground vehicles, including tanks, trains, and trucks.

Amazingly, the Tuskegee Airmen flew two hundred bomber escort missions without losing a single bomber to enemy attacks. They brought home 150 Distinguished Flying Crosses and Legions of Merit. But along with their triumph came tragedy. Sixty-six Tuskegee Airmen were killed in action and another thirty-two were captured and became prisoners of war.

After Germany surrendered on May 8, 1945, the 332nd Fighter Group was disbanded. Some Tuskegee Airmen stayed in the military and fought in later wars. Tuskegee Airman Charles McGee compiled an exemplary military career that spanned thirty years. In addition to fighting in World War II, McGee served in Korea and Vietnam. He achieved the highest three-war total of fighter missions of any air force aviator—409 missions.

Japan surrendered on August 14, ending World War II. Inspired by the group's magnificent contribution to the war effort, President Harry S. Truman announced Executive Order 9981 on July 26, 1948. Calling for "equality of treatment and opportunity in the armed forces regardless of race," the act led to the end of segregation in the armed forces. The Tuskegee Airmen have gone down in history as a primary reason the armed forces stopped segregation before the nation did.

ROCKET MAN COMES TO ALABAMA

1950

It may have seemed a strange situation. A man from Germany plunked down in the humid Deep South in the 1950s. But Wernher von Braun went on to become the "rocket man" who would forge the American space program and lead the team that blasted Americans into space and to the moon.

Along the way, von Braun and his team transformed the cotton fields of Huntsville, Alabama, his home for the next twenty years, into a landmark of space exploration. When von Braun arrived, the tiny Alabama town with a population of 15,000 called itself the "Watercress Capital of the World."

Today, it is forever known as the place where America's space program was born. It's not surprising that Huntsville is also home to one of the earth's largest space museums and attractions—the U.S. Space & Rocket Center. It is also the site of the U.S. Space Camp, where more than a half-million young people and adults from all 50 states and dozens of foreign counties have studied space and learned what it's like to be an astronaut.

Von Braun himself was fascinated with space and rockets as a child. Born into an aristocratic family on March 23, 1912, von Braun inherited the title of baron at birth. His birthplace was in Wirsitz, a small town in Prussia that was part of Germany at the time but is now in present-day Poland.

His father, Baron Magnus Alexander Maxmilian von Braun, was a top county official and his mother was Baroness Emmy von Quistorp von Braun. The family owned several estates and moved often when von Braun was growing up as his father changed jobs. During World War I, his father served as press secretary to the chancellor but resigned when Adolf Hitler was appointed chancellor.

An intelligent child, von Braun was a talented pianist and cellist who wrote his own compositions. Showing an early interest in jet propulsion, the twelve-year-old built a wagon powered by skyrockets that reportedly zoomed down a Berlin street and earned the boy a trip to the local police station. Von Braun seems to have come by his space interest naturally. His mother was an amateur astronomer who enjoyed scanning the heavens with a telescope and encouraged her son's celestial fascination. In school, he excelled at math and physics and enjoyed books on rockets and space travel by authors like Jules Verne and H. G. Wells.

Graduating from the Charlottenburg Institute of Technology in 1932 at age twenty, von Braun helped other Berlin rocket enthusiasts build small liquid-fueled rockets. Some of these friends would later join von Braun in developing the V-2 rocket and would travel with him to America. Known as the Society for Space Travel, the group was offered funding by the German Army to further their rocket work. That's how the young man became involved in designing and building weaponized rockets as a civilian employee. He had no idea that Germany would soon be at war and that his research might be used for a more deadly purpose.

At age twenty-two, von Braun received a doctorate in physics from the Friedrich-Wilhelms University of Berlin. He and his colleagues also were successful in launching liquid-fueled rockets. As a result, the German air force, the Luftwaffe, offered the group more than a million dollars to develop a rocket-powered fighter plane. To meet his compulsory military requirement, von Braun became a Luftwaffe cadet in 1936 and was trained to fly military aircraft. He also became a member of the Nazi Party on December 1, 1938, and the Schustzstaffel or SS, the paramilitary arm of the Nazi Party, in May 1940. Historians say that von Braun wasn't a supporter of Nazi politics but joined the groups because he wanted to be allowed to continue working to build rockets to take humans into space.

Asked to develop a more advanced military rocket, von Braun chose to set up a secret site on a Baltic island where his grandfather used to hunt ducks. Moving to Peenemunde on the island of Usedom, the engineers focused on building rockets as weapons using thousands of forced laborers to build the V-2 rocket. The world's first ballistic missile, the V-2 was forty-six feet tall, had a range of about two hundred miles, and carried a 2,200-pound warhead. Beginning in late summer 1944, the missiles were launched against London, Paris, Belgium, and the Netherlands. More than seven thousand people, mostly civilians, died from about 3,100 V-2 launches. Another twelve thousand or more forced laborers—Russian, French, and Polish prisoners of war—died as a result of the horrible working and living conditions at the V-2 plant.

Peaceful uses such as space travel were forbidden subjects for von Braun and fellow engineers. In fact, von Braun was jailed in March 1944 by the German secret police, the Gestapo. He was accused of treason because he had dared make comments about wanting to work on space travel and perhaps escaping to England to do so. Von Braun was released in May because he was a valuable asset for Nazi Germany.

When the war ended, von Braun and his brother Magnus and other colleagues surrendered to American forces on May 2, 1945. Von Braun is credited with arranging the surrender of five hundred of his top rocket scientists, along with plans and test vehicles to the Americans. The space scientists reasoned that their work would be better supported and appreciated in the United States than in the Soviet Union or Great Britain. And U.S. military leaders were eager to prevent von Braun and the others from falling into Soviet hands to be used for their superior knowledge.

The group was initially taken to Fort Bliss, Texas, to learn English and to train Americans in rocket science. Von Braun's travel was restricted, and he was often under the surveillance of the Central Intelligence Agency in fear of his being kidnapped by the Soviet Union or China. That ban was lifted in 1955 when von Braun and more than one hundred of his fellow Germans became American citizens in ceremonies in Huntsville.

"This is the happiest and most significant day in my life," von Braun said at the time. "I must say we all became American citizens in our hearts long ago."

At first hesitant to interact with folks in Huntsville, von Braun urged his fellow countrymen to enjoy the Southern hospitality of their new home. As a result, church gatherings and dinner parties began featuring German dishes with warm invitations to the foreigners. Local grocery stories began carrying German-made goods. During his two decades in Huntsville, von Braun helped form the Huntsville Symphony Orchestra and helped build the Rocket City Astronomical Observatory and Planetarium. He also spoke out against the state's Jim Crow laws and was a strong advocate for hiring blacks and other minorities.

The Huntsville group was an important contributor to America's efforts during the Cold War arms race after World War II. Russia was aggressively building intercontinental ballistic missiles and nuclear weapons even as the German team's work led to the creation of the Redstone missile in 1954. The Redstone rocket was a larger, more powerful, and more reliable version of the V-2.

More importantly to him, von Braun led the United States in the space race. In 1957, the world was stunned when the Soviet Union put the first satellites into orbit. Sputnik I was launched in October and Sputnik II in November, signaling the start of the space race between the United States and the Soviet Union.

On January 31, 1958, the United States launched its first satellite, Explorer I, into orbit. When the National Aeronautics and Space Administration (NASA) was created in 1958, von Braun became the first director of the Marshall Space Flight Center. On May 5, 1961, a Redstone rocket carried astronaut Alan Sheppard on a suborbital flight, three weeks after Soviet cosmonaut Yuri Gagarin orbited the earth one revolution.

Between 1968 and 1972, the Apollo program successfully orbited one mission around the earth, three missions around the moon, and landed seven missions on the moon. The 1969 Apollo 11 mission made the first landing on the moon, turning von Braun's long-time dream into a reality. Von Braun and his engineers were honored with a hero's celebration in Huntsville.

Von Braun also helped popularize the idea of space exploration with the American public. He was interviewed in magazine articles and was frequently a guest speaker, promoting the importance of the space program. He consulted with Walt Disney on a television show about space and appeared in three episodes of the show. He also acted as a consultant on attractions at Disneyland and Disney World.

When he was appointed NASA's deputy associate administrator in 1970, von Braun and his family moved to Alexandria, Virginia. He left NASA in 1972 to join Fairchild Industries in Germantown,

Maryland. Von Braun retired from Fairchild in 1977 because he had cancer. He died June 16, 1977, and was buried at Ivy Hill Cemetery in Alexandria. Von Braun's legacy lives on in Alabama where aerospace continues to be a key industry in the state's economic development.

HANK WILLIAMS'S FUNERAL

1953

The year 1953 started off on a sad note for many country music fans. Shortly after celebrating the New Year, mourners began flocking to Montgomery. They lined the streets and congregated outside a boardinghouse where a silver casket sat. So many people came to pay tribute that the funeral couldn't be held in a church. The service had to be moved to the biggest facility in town, the Municipal Auditorium.

Ironically, that was the very auditorium where the fallen star had performed so many times. Now it was where Hank Williams, the Drifting Cowboy, would be bade farewell for his last journey.

On Sunday afternoon, January 4, 1953, an estimated 25,000 came to Montgomery for the funeral of Hank Williams. It was a record crowd for the city that has never been surpassed.

Only 2,750 were able to get inside the City Auditorium. The balcony of the segregated facility was set aside for black mourners and about 200 of them crowded in. The rest of the folks listened as the funeral was broadcast on a PA system outside in the streets and in Lister Hill Park or tuned in as radio stations carried the funeral service.

Grand Ole Opry stars arrived in a special chartered plane. Among the Opry entertainers were Jimmy Dickens, Carl Smith, Webb Pierce, Bill Monroe, Ray Price, and June Carter. Loads of flowers were delivered, including two guitar-shaped floral arrangements that stood on each side of the coffin. Hitching a ride to Montgomery for his son's funeral, Hank's father Lon Williams spent his last $5 for flowers at Rosemont Gardens where employees were working overtime to fill orders pouring in from around the nation. Rosemont made a big bouquet for the elder Williams, despite the meager money he had.

At 1:00 p.m., the casket was brought in and opened at 1:15. Dressed in a white cowboy stage outfit, Hank clutched a tiny white Bible in his hand. Hank's band, the Drifting Cowboys, stood by as a guard of honor. Hundreds filed by to pay their respects.

At 2:30 p.m., the auditorium doors were closed, and the service started with Ernest Tubb singing "Beyond the Sunset." A gospel quartet, the Statesmen, who would later sing at Elvis's funeral, sang "Precious Memories." Possibly the only black quartet to perform at a prominent white funeral in Alabama prior to the civil rights era, the Southwind Singers sang "My Record Will Be There."

Roy Acuff performed Hank's popular song, "I Saw the Light." Honoring a promise he had made with Hank that whoever went first, the other would sing at his funeral, Red Foley sang "Peace in the Valley," his voice quavering and tears running down his face. Four women fainted during the service.

"I can't preach his funeral," Dr. Henry Lyon, pastor of the biggest Baptist church in Montgomery, told the gathering. "His eulogy was in his musical works."

Hank Williams was only twenty-nine years old when he died. How did such a young man leave such a lasting legacy and draw so many important and everyday folks to his funeral?

Born near Georgiana, Alabama, on September 17, 1923, Hiriam (as spelled on his birth certificate) "Hank" Williams was the second child of Lon and Lillie Williams. His father was a World War I veteran who was hospitalized for war stress most of the boy's early life. A small child afflicted with spina bifida, Williams seemed drawn to music from the beginning, singing in church choirs as a child. One of his best friends was Rufus Payne, a black street musician known as "Tee-Tot." Williams later credited Payne with giving him "all the music training I ever had."

Williams and his mother moved to Montgomery in 1937. He was only fourteen when he entered an amateur talent contest at The Empire Theater and won $15 for first place for singing his original "WPA Blues." At age sixteen, Williams quit school and turned to his music career with a vengeance. A regular on local radio shows, he played at almost every high school auditorium, honky tonk, and fair in the area, backed by his band, the Drifting Cowboys.

In 1944, Williams married Audrey Mae Sheppard, an Alabama country girl with a two-year-old daughter from a previous marriage. Learning to play stand-up bass, Audrey joined the band and made some recordings herself. But it was Hank that the fans clamored for. In all, Williams recorded 225 songs and wrote 128 of them. Under the pseudonym "Luke the Drifter," he tried to work out his demons in gospel themes and a series of recitations.

On a warm night in June 1949, Williams reached the pinnacle—his debut at Ryman Auditorium for the Grand Ole Opry. Less than four years later, he would be gone.

By mid-1952, his life was on the skids. Audrey filed for divorce and took their son, Randall Hank Williams Jr. Wracked with back pain, Williams tried to ease his misery with whiskey and morphine, prescribed and often administered by doctors. The Opry fired him for showing up drunk or not showing up at all.

Making a stab at salvation, he married young Billie Jean Jones, the daughter of a cop. The marriage was later proven to be invalid because Billie Jean's previous divorce hadn't been finalized when she and Hank married. He also signed a pre-birth custody agreement with Bobbie Jett, a Nashville secretary carrying his child. Williams would have full custody of the baby and pay Jett's way to California.

The last Sunday in December 1952, Hank performed for a Musicians Union meeting. The next Sunday would be his funeral.

Slumped in the backseat of a baby blue Cadillac speeding through a dark night, Hank Williams drew his last breath. The country music legend was on his way to a concert in Canton, Ohio. Somewhere in West Virginia, Williams' young driver became worried about the lifeless body draped in a navy blue overcoat in the backseat. By then it was too late.

Carried into an emergency room, Williams was pronounced dead on January 1, 1953. His heart had given out after years of alcohol and prescription drug abuse.

Hank is buried in Oakwood Cemetery in Montgomery. It seems somehow appropriate given the confused tragedy of his life that Hank's last journey wasn't quite his last. On January 17, 1953, his casket was dug up and moved to a bigger section of the cemetery in a family plot his mother bought. The work was done by lamplight after midnight because Hank's grave was seldom without visitors.

But strange happenings were still to come. The tale of Jett Williams seems a bizarre postscript to Hank's life.

Her unbelievable story sounds like the improbable gist of a country music song that might have been written by old Hank. Born to Bobbie Jett five days after Williams' death, the baby was adopted by Hank's mother and named Cathy Yvonne, the middle name from the Williams's hit "Jambalaya."

Two months after the adoption was finalized, Lillian Williams died. The rest of the family turned the young girl over as a ward of the state and had her birth records sealed. Placed in a series of foster homes, she was eventually adopted by a couple in Mobile. But when she turned twenty-one, the young lady got a surprise. A check for $3,000 arrived from Williams's estate. Unknown to his other family, Hank had made provisions for his daughter to receive money on her twenty-first birthday, and somehow that check had slipped through.

That set the daughter on a journey to find out the truth about her heritage. Discovering the pre-birth custody agreement that would have given Williams full custody of the child, the young woman was eventually awarded half of her father's estate and her share of her father's songs from 1985 forward. She legally changed her name to "Jett Williams" and is now a performer who dresses on stage much as her father did and sings his songs. She turned her story into the autobiography, *Ain't Nothing As Sweet As My Baby: The Story of Hank Williams's Lost Daughter*.

Hank's fans still find their way to Montgomery to see his life-size statue downtown, the Cadillac where he died at the Hank Williams Museum, and his grave. In 1991, singer Alan Jackson penned a tribute to Hank called "Midnight in Montgomery" and filmed a video at the gravesite about a memorable meeting with a tall mournful stranger in a cowboy hat.

> 'Cause it's midnight in Montgomery
> Just hear that whippoorwill
> See the stars light up the purple sky
> Feel that lonesome chill
> When the wind it's right, you'll hear his songs

HANK WILLIAMS'S FUNERAL

Smell whiskey in the air
Midnight in Montgomery . . .
Hank's always singing there.

METEORITE HITS WOMAN

1954

Taking a nap on her couch, a Sylacauga woman got a rude awakening. Crashing through the roof of her home, an eight-and-half-pound meteorite bounced off a console radio and smashed into the woman's hand and hip.

It is the only confirmed occurrence of an extraterrestrial hitting a human.

The event on November 30, 1954, caused a flurry of media coverage, an air force investigation, a bidding war, and a lawsuit. Today, the hunk of space stone—known as Hodges Meteorite—is on display at the Alabama Museum of Natural History at the University of Alabama.

When the meteorite hit and she was jolted awake by the pain and noise, thirty-one-year-old Ann Hodges first thought a gas space heater had exploded and blasted something at her. Then she saw the grapefruit-sized rock on the floor and worried that children must have thrown it at the house. Her mother, Ida Franklin, rushed outside and saw nothing but a black cloud in the sky—and a gaping hole in the roof.

People in Alabama and nearby states reported seeing a fireball streaking through the sky at about the same time. Neighbors said they saw the falling star, followed by an explosion and billowing smoke. Most onlookers thought it must have been an airplane crash.

Geologists said the loud noise was likely a sonic boom created by the meteorite as it traveled many times the speed of sound.

Police were summoned, and reporters flocked to the scene. Traffic jams blocked the Oak Grove community where Hodges lived. Ironically, across the road from Hodges's white-frame house was the Comet Drive-in Theater with its neon sign showing a comet blasting toward the heavens.

Examined by local doctor Moody Jacobs, Hodges was determined to have no permanent damage. Her hip and hand were swollen and painful, with a grapefruit-sized bruise on her hip. But her life was never the same.

Conducting fieldwork in the area at the time, geologist George Swindel identified the object as a meteorite and gave it to officers from Maxwell Field. Officers took it to air force intelligence authorities for analysis. With the Cold War and fears of invasions in the 1950s, government officials wanted to be sure America hadn't been hit with some kind of missile. After being determined to really be an outer space object, the meteorite was turned over to the Smithsonian Institution.

Then the lawsuits started.

If it came from outer space and was the only one to hit a human, then it must be valuable, people reasoned. Ann Hodges and her husband, Eugene Hewlett Hodges, wanted the meteorite back so that they could sell it. Birdie Guy, the landlady who owned the home where Hodges was hit, figured she owned the rock since it landed in her house. Guy also reckoned that she would need the money to repair the house. Siding with her, Guy's attorney cited legal precedent that said meteorites were the property of the landowner. Guy sued for possession of the rock. The Hodges countersued.

The landlady and renters finally came to an agreement. After multiple appeals won by Guy, the Hodges paid Guy $500 for the meteorite, which by then wasn't worth much because much of its curiosity factor had faded. Although Hodges had more than her fifteen minutes of fame, the couple certainly didn't get rich.

Besieged by the media, Hodges was featured in *Life* magazine, as well as many other newspapers and magazines around the nation. She also appeared on Gary Moore's popular TV show, *I've Got a Secret*. But, less than two years later, it was all over. After turning down an earlier offer from the Smithsonian Institution because her husband didn't think it was enough money, Hodges eventually donated the meteorite—against her husband's wishes—to the Alabama Museum of Natural History.

Citing the unexpected impact on their lives and marriage by the meteorite, the Hodges separated in 1964. Both said they wished the space rock had never entered their orbit. After declining health and years in a nursing home, Ann Hodges died of kidney failure in 1972. She was only forty-nine. She is buried in Charity Baptist Church cemetery in Hazel Green.

The meteorite itself is still on display underneath a glass case at the Alabama Museum of Natural History. The seven-inch-by-five-inch-by-five-inch rock is covered with a thick black coating from its blazing entry. It has several chips and a patch of tar from the Hodges' roof.

Meteorites in space may travel at a rate of more than 30,000 miles per hour, officials said. Smaller ones break up and are slowed down and burned as they enter the earth's atmosphere. Known as a chondrite, the Hodges Meteorite was formed during the early years of the solar system, about four to five billion years ago. It was traveling several hundred miles an hour when it struck the house.

Most likely, geologists say, the stone was a fragment from a meteorite that probably weighed more than 150 pounds when it entered the earth's atmosphere. On May 22, 2010, the city of Oak Grove dedicated a historical marker at the site of the meteorite strike.

Another fragment from the same stone had a much happier ending for the man who found it.

A farmer who lived near the Hodges, Julius McKinney, was driving a mule-drawn wagon with a load of firewood about two miles from the Hodges's home the day after the famed meteorite fell to earth. McKinney came upon a large black rock in the middle of the road, causing his mules to balk. Moving the strange rock to the side of the road, McKinney went on home. After hearing about the Hodges uproar, McKinney went back to the site that night, loaded up the rock, and took it home for his children to play with.

Experts confirmed that the three-pound rock had split off from the Hodges meteorite when it burned through the atmosphere. When McKinney's postman heard about the discovery, he helped McKinney find a lawyer to negotiate a deal with the Smithsonian for the object.

Although McKinney never revealed what he was paid, he seemed to come out far ahead of the Hodges when the star fell on Alabama. McKinney allows that he got enough money to buy a new house and a car.

ROSA PARKS REFUSES TO GIVE UP HER BUS SEAT

1955

She was a seamstress, riding a bus home from a hard day's work in Montgomery. But that memorable journey propelled her straight into history.

The quiet, unassuming woman who was "tired of giving in" became the fuse that ignited the massive Montgomery bus boycott and made Rosa Parks into "the mother of the modern day civil rights movement."

The forty-two-year-old African-American woman was on her way home from work at a downtown department store. Bespectacled, her hair pulled back tightly, Parks didn't look like someone wanting to cause trouble. But when trouble came her way that day, Parks didn't flinch.

Boarding the bus on that chilly December day, she sank down wearily in the first row of the black section of the public bus. A widely held myth says that Parks sat in the front of the bus, behind the driver. In truth, she took her seat in the first row of the black section. The first five rows were empty but they were marked WHITES ONLY. It was against the law for blacks to sit there.

At the next bus stop at the old Empire Theatre, a crowd of people got on the bus—too many riders for the seats available. It was "expected" that black passengers would know their place and get up to give their seats to white riders. They didn't. So the driver walked back to the "black section" to move Parks and three other black passengers so that white riders could sit.

At first, all four didn't budge. Then, after warnings from the driver, three stood and moved. Only Parks remained. She was arrested, fingerprinted, put behind bars, then later bailed out. But that was the beginning of the end of Jim Crow segregation. Parks later wrote that the momentous event was not "scripted" and could not have been planned in advance.

"But throughout the community organizations in Montgomery," she wrote, "we had been planning for freedom all of our lives."

Although she was worn out, Parks later wrote, fatigue was not the reason she refused to move. "People always say that I didn't give up my seat because I was tired, but that isn't true," she wrote. "No, the only tired I was, was tired of giving in."

At that time, blacks were being treated as second-class citizens in every aspect of public life. They faced segregated schools, water fountains, lunch counters, bathrooms, elevators, buses, cabs, and on and on. Black Americans had to sit in the back of buses.

Parks's quiet courage helped bring to the forefront a young Montgomery preacher, the Rev. Martin Luther King Jr., who would go on to galvanize the nation. And the boycott of the busy bus system in the days that followed her arrest showed how nonviolence could be effective against oppression.

The boycott began December 5, 1955, and lasted 381 days until the U.S. Supreme Court struck down segregation laws. At the time, many people thought the boycott would last a week. It continued thirteen months, and the bus companies almost went bankrupt. Buses were empty because blacks stopped riding. All areas of life were impacted by the boycott.

Large station wagons transported boycotters to and from work. Many blacks chose to walk, even in the cold temperatures. White people joined in to offer their services and their vehicles to keep the boycott going.

The lives of Parks and her husband, Raymond, also were impacted in ways they never expected. "I felt the Lord would give me the strength to endure whatever I had to face," Parks wrote in her 1994 memoir *Quiet Strength*.

Born February 4, 1913, in Tuskegee, Alabama, Rosa McCauley Parks grew up on a farm. Her father, James McCauley, was a carpenter. Her mother, Leona McCauley, had been a teacher before Rosa was born. Life was not easy for the family. Her father was often gone for months at a time for work.

When Rosa was two, she and her parents moved to a farm with her grandfather and grandma Rose. After her mother had another baby named Sylvester, Rosa's parents split, and Rosa didn't see her father again until she was an adult. Rosa's mother worked at a school and, because the family didn't have a car, lived close to it and came home only on weekends. Rosa was raised mainly by her grandparents.

When she was six, Rosa started school in a tiny one-room schoolhouse for black children. The school closed when Rosa was eleven, but her mother took a second job as a maid and paid for Rosa to attend a private school for black girls—the Montgomery Industrial School. Staying with an aunt in Montgomery, Rosa studied core subjects as well as cooking and sewing, which she most enjoyed. Rosa also learned the hard life of segregation in Montgomery.

When Rosa was in the ninth grade, her private school closed, and she began attending a black public junior high school. Later, she went to the only black high school around and dreamed of becoming a nurse or a teacher. But family life stopped those plans. When Rosa was in the eleventh grade, her grandmother got sick, and Rosa went home to take care of her until she died. Then Rosa's mother got sick, and the girl tended to her, too. That meant, of course, that Rosa had to drop out of school. "It was just something that had to be done," she later said.

At age eighteen, Rosa met the man who would change her life. Ten years older than she was, Raymond Parks was a barber who was active in community life and in the National Association for the Advancement of Colored People fighting for civil rights. Two years after meeting, the pair married in 1932. Raymond Parks encouraged his young wife to get her high school diploma. Rosa went back to high school and graduated when she was twenty.

Raymond also encouraged Rosa to learn about the NAACP. She attended a meeting one night in 1943 and was soon the group's secretary. Realizing that voting meant power, Rosa joined the Montgomery Voters League and helped blacks register to vote.

Although blacks had the right to vote in Alabama, rules often kept them from exercising that right. For example, blacks had specific times when they could register to vote—usually in the middle of a workday. Since they didn't own land, blacks also had to take a test before they could register to vote, and the test was definitely designed to exclude blacks from voting. Questions were often impossible to answer: How many bubbles are in a bar of soap? How high is up?

Even though Rosa was well educated, it took her three tries before she passed the test.

In 1943, Rosa had a terrible experience on a Montgomery bus with the same driver she would encounter again twelve years later.

Entering the bus through the front door, Rosa was ordered to get off the bus and then get on again using the back door. Rosa refused. The driver grabbed her and shoved her toward the door. This time, Rosa got off the bus and did not get back on. But she remembered the face of the driver, and when they had an encounter again in 1955, Rosa didn't back down.

When Rosa Parks and bus driver James Blake came face to face again on December 1, 1955, Parks was arrested. Her husband and friends paid the $100 to bail her out—a great deal of money at the time. On December 5, Rosa went to court where she was found guilty and ordered to pay a $14 fine. Her attorney Fred Gray said that the city's bus laws were unjust, that Parks would not pay the fine, and that he would ask the U.S. Supreme Court to review her case. Furthermore, blacks would boycott Montgomery buses. On November 13, 1956, the Supreme Court ruled that segregation on city buses in Alabama was unconstitutional. On December 21, 1956, the law changed, and black Americans could sit wherever they wanted on city buses.

But life became so difficult for Parks and her husband in Montgomery that they moved in 1957 to Detroit where her brother lived. Parks left Montgomery because of threats on her life and because she couldn't get a job. Her husband had a nervous breakdown. In Detroit, Rosa Parks got a job as a seamstress in a clothing factory. She later became an assistant to black Congressman John Conyers.

Raymond Parks died in 1977 in Detroit. Rosa Parks continued living there and spent the rest of her life traveling the world and speaking about education, youth development, and racial harmony. She also helped found the Rosa and Raymond Parks Institute for Self-Development in 1987. The institute prepares young blacks for leadership positions in the workplace and the community.

Parks died at age ninety-two on October 24, 2005. For two days, her coffin was placed inside the U.S. Capitol in Washington D.C., where people could pay their respects to the civil rights pioneer. Parks was the first woman to receive this honor usually reserved for presidents and war heroes. She was buried in a Detroit cemetery.

On the day of her funeral, flags around the nation were flown at half-mast, and the front seats of buses in Montgomery and other cities were left empty to honor her memory and years of struggle. Parks had no children born to her but has said, "I consider all children as mine."

TO SAVE A MOCKINGBIRD

1956

On a bitter cold Christmas Eve in 1956, a homesick young woman couldn't get off work to spend the holidays with her family in Alabama. Unhappy about a book she had spent years writing, the woman knew that her dingy New York flat was no place to be alone. She was glad to accept an invitation to share the festivities with a Manhattan couple and their two young sons.

When Christmas morning arrived, the guest was rousted out of bed by the youngsters wanting to open presents. Knowing that money was scarce, the hosts and their visitor had set a tradition of limiting gifts to each other. Instead, they relied on creativity and careful searching to find low-cost treasures for the holiday exchange.

Watching the children and parents unwrap their gifts, the Christmas guest noticed that nothing was being placed by her chair for her excited unveiling. "My disappointment was growing steadily," she later wrote. "But I tried not to show it."

The family took their time, happily exclaiming over the budget gems she had found them—a print for him, a book for her. Finally, the couple told their guest to look on the decorated Christmas tree. "We haven't forgotten you," they said. There, peeking among the branches of the festive tree was a small white envelope with her name on it.

Opening it, the struggling writer saw the words: "You have one year off from your job to write whatever you please. Merry Christmas."

It wasn't a joke. These friends had saved enough money and had enough faith in the tormented novelist that they wanted to give her the freedom to write without the harassments of a regular job or the worry of paying bills.

"I went to the window, stunned by the day's miracle," she later wrote in an article, "Christmas to Me," published in *McCall's* magazine in December 1961. "A full, fair chance for a new life. Not given me by an act of generosity, but by an act of love. Our faith in you was really all I had heard them say. I would do my best not to fail them."

And, of course, the guest did not fail her supportive friends. Harper Lee went on to pen one of the greatest novels ever written— *To Kill a Mockingbird.*

Published in 1960, the Pulitzer Prize–winning book has sold more than 30 million copies and was voted in 1999 the "Best Novel of the Century" in a poll by the *Library Journal.* A 1962 movie adaptation of the book won three Academy Awards, including best actor for Gregory Peck.

Lee was thirty-four when her work was published. It has remained her only novel.

How did a young Alabama woman create such an amazingly successful book? She wrote about what she knew.

Born April 28, 1926, in Monroeville, Alabama, Nelle Harper Lee was the youngest child of Frances Cunningham Finch Lee and Amasa Coleman Lee, a lawyer. She had a brother and two sisters and a next-door neighbor who would play a very important part in her life and writing career.

"We had to use our own devices in our play, for our entertainment. We didn't have much money," Lee said in a 1965 interview. "We didn't have toys, nothing was done for us, so the result was that we lived in our imagination most of the time. We devised things; we were readers, and we would transfer everything we had seen on the printed page to the backyard in the form of high drama."

A tomboy interested in reading and writing even as a child, Lee and her neighbor were thrilled when her father gave them an old Underwood typewriter. Friends since kindergarten, the two playmates began writing original stories. Drawn together by "an apartness" they recognized in each other, Lee and Truman Capote let their creativity soar. Capote was living with his aunts and uncles in Monroeville and moved to New York City in the third grade to join his mother and stepfather. But he returned to Monroeville for summers and was said to be the inspiration for Dill in *To Kill a Mockingbird*.

Before her father became a title lawyer, he had defended two black men accused of murdering a white storekeeper. Both clients, a father and son, were found guilty and hanged. Her father never practiced criminal law again. In her book, Lee writes about a dedicated widowed attorney who defends a black man accused of raping a white woman. An all-white, male jury finds the black man guilty and he dies.

After Lee graduated from Monroeville high school, she attended Huntingdon College in Montgomery from 1944 through 1945. In 1945, she transferred to the University of Alabama in Tuscaloosa to study law. She left in 1949 without completing her degree and moved to New York to pursue a literary career. To pay the bills, Lee got a job as an airline reservations clerk.

The story goes that in 1957 Lee got so fed up with the book she had been writing that she threw it out her apartment window into the dirty snow below. The manuscript might have been lost in the winter debris, but a telephone conversation with her editor sent Lee scurrying outside to tearfully gather the discarded pages.

After the "year off" Christmas present from her friends, Michael and Joy Brown, Lee quit her job and began writing as soon as she got out of bed each morning. Fortified by coffee, she often wrote until after midnight. Her output soared, and Lee started working with Tay Hofoff, an editor at J. B. Lippincott. After almost three years of rewriting, the work was finally ready for publication. The author chose the name "Harper Lee" on the cover because she didn't want to be incorrectly identified as "Nellie." Her first name, Nelle, is actually her grandmother's name spelled backward.

Set in the 1930s make-believe Alabama town of Maycomb, *To Kill a Mockingbird* resolves around tomboy Scout, the daughter of respected small-town Alabama attorney Atticus Finch. "It was a tired old town when I first knew it," Lee described in the first chapter of her book. "In rainy weather, the streets turned to red slop. Grass grew on the sidewalks. The courthouse sagged in the square."

Scout's father decides to defend a black man, Tom Robinson, who is accused of raping a poor white girl, Mayella Ewell. It's not a happily-ever-after book because Atticus loses the case, Tom tries to escape, and he is shot dead. The true rapist goes after Finch's two children, and they are saved by the heroism of the town reclusive boogeyman—Boo Radley.

The title? "Mockingbirds don't do one thing but make music for us to enjoy," Lee wrote in her novel. "They don't eat up people's gardens, don't nest in corncribs, they don't do one thing but sing their hearts out for us. That's why it's a sin to kill a mockingbird."

The book was an immediate and astounding success, something that Lee did not expect. She did not enjoy the celebrity limelight and rejected interview requests, honorary degrees, and anything else that brought attention to her.

"It was like being hit over the head and knocked out cold," Lee said, acknowledging that all the attention "was frightening."

With the exception of a few short essays, Lee has published no further writings. She did work on a second novel, *The Long Goodbye*, but never finished it. She also began a book, *The Reverend*, in the mid-1980s, about an Alabama serial murderer but also put it aside.

What she did do was go to Kansas in the 1960s with her old buddy Truman Capote to serve as "assistant researchist" for his book *In Cold Blood.* Published in 1966, Capote's book was declared a masterpiece. Capote dedicated the book to Lee and credited her with "secretarial work" and with befriending some of the people he wanted to interview. By then, of course, Capote was enormously successful with works such as *Other Voices, Other Rooms* in 1948 and *Breakfast at Tiffany's* in 1958.

While Capote mingled with the rich and famous, Lee divided her time between a quiet summer apartment in New York and a Monroeville home with her older sister Alice. After years of alcohol and drugs, Capote self-destructed and died at fifty-nine in 1984. Lee said at the time that she hadn't heard from her old friend in years.

Lee now lives full-time in Monroeville in a sheltered housing complex after suffering a stroke. Lee is often seen out and about town, but most people know better than to disturb her. "Hell no," Lee once wrote in answer to an interviewer's request.

"When you're at the top," she once told her cousin Dickie Williams, "there is only one way to go."

LETTER FROM BIRMINGHAM JAIL

1963

Locked in solitary confinement in Birmingham jail, the inmate was slipped a newspaper. Hungrily reading it, the prisoner saw a printed advertisement of a letter aimed directly at him.

Angry and indignant, the jailed man wanted to answer his critics' letter, so he began scrawling in the margins of the newspaper. That was the start of a writing that would eventually be translated into more than forty languages and become the cornerstone for the civil rights movement and for nonviolent protests around the world.

On April 16, 1963, Dr. Martin Luther King Jr. wrote his famed "Letter from Birmingham Jail."

"There are two types of laws, just and unjust," King wrote from his narrow jail cell on Easter weekend. "One has a moral responsibility to disobey unjust laws."

Following his conscience and doing just that is what landed thirty-four-year-old King in jail in the first place.

In the 1960s, Birmingham was one of the most rigidly segregated cities in the nation. Although African Americans made up 40 percent of the city's population, they knew "their place" and what would happen if they didn't stay in it. The large industrial city had become a symbol of police brutality under Commissioner of Public Safety Eugene "Bull" Connor. Violent images captured snarling police dogs and high-powered fire hoses turned on civil rights demonstrators.

Black churches and homes of civil rights leaders were bombed. A black man was castrated, then dumped on a country road. Fear ruled the city, presided over by governor George Wallace whose inauguration vow had been "segregation now, segregation tomorrow, segregation forever!"

That is what brought King to Birmingham.

Spurred by the success of the Montgomery bus boycott, Birmingham residents were determined to gain equal rights and overturn the reign of Bull Connor. Birmingham already had a dedicated freedom fighter right in its midst. The Rev. Fred Shuttlesworth had organized the Alabama Christian Movement for Human Rights in 1956. The organization soon became one of the eighty-five affiliations of the Southern Christian Leadership Conference.

Shuttlesworth was already paying the price for his civil rights work. His home had been bombed and totally destroyed. His church, Bethel Baptist, had been dynamited. In 1957, Shuttlesworth and his wife were mobbed, beaten, and stabbed. They were jailed eight times for their protests.

That is the setting when King decided to join efforts in Birmingham. He later wrote, "We believed that while a campaign in Birmingham would surely be the toughest fight of our civil rights careers, it could, if successful, break the back of segregation all over the nation."

The focus of the Birmingham struggle, King and other leaders decided, would be the boycott of the business community. "We knew that the Negro population had sufficient buying power so that its withdrawal could make the difference between profit and loss for many businesses," King wrote in his autobiography.

Meeting in Room 30 of the Gaston Motel, King and his group plotted their strategy. The starting date, they decided, would be the second biggest shopping season of the year—Easter. Sit-ins with freedom songs kicked off the Birmingham campaign. And it started rather peacefully with few arrests.

Why sing? King explained in his autobiography that the freedom songs were "the soul of the movement. They are adaptations of the songs the slaves sang—the sorrow songs, the shouts for joy, the battle hymns, and the anthems of our movement. . . . We sing the freedom songs for the same reason the slaves sang them, because we too are in bondage and the songs add hope to our determination that, 'We shall overcome. Black and white together, we shall overcome someday.'"

In his jailhouse letter, King also addressed critics who called him an outsider. "No Negro, in fact, no American, is an outsider when he goes to any community to aid the cause of freedom and justice. . . . Injustice anywhere is a threat to justice everywhere."

How did King end up in jail? By the end of the first three days of Birmingham lunch counter sit-ins, there had been thirty-five arrests. On April 6, 1963, protestors marched on city hall, and the marches and business boycotts increased. On April 10, city government obtained a court injunction for the protestors to cease their activities until a court decided their legal right to demonstrate. Two days later, the protestors did something unheard of—they disobeyed the court order, precisely what Henry David Thoreau had written about in his *Civil Disobedience,* published in 1849.

On Good Friday, April 12, King and fellow civil rights activist Ralph Abernathy took the next step, knowing full well that they would be arrested. The men also knew that they might spend lengthy time in jail because the bail bondsman they had been using for quick releases had been notified by the city that his financial assets were insufficient and he would be unable to continue.

Deciding to march anyway, King and Abernathy and others were arrested. King was thrown in solitary confinement, unable to communicate with anyone, even his lawyer. King spent nine days in the Birmingham jail.

On April 12, eight local white clergymen wrote an open letter printed in the *Birmingham News* denouncing King and demanding an end to the demonstrations. The ministers argued that the battle against racial segregation should be fought solely in the courts, not in the streets. Using what scraps of paper he could get, King crafted a lengthy response that his attorneys were later able to smuggle out of the jail in installments.

"Never before have I written so long a letter," King wrote. "I can assure you that it would have been much shorter if I had been writing from a comfortable desk, but what else can one do when he is alone in a narrow jail cell, other than write long letters, think long thoughts, and pray long prayers?"

Describing the "shameful humiliation" and "inexpressible cruelties" of American slavery, King said that black Americans had already waited centuries "for our constitutional and God-given rights. . . . We still creep at horse-and-buggy pace toward gaining a cup of coffee at a lunch counter."

The letter became an instruction manual for people everywhere to stand up to injustice through nonviolent direct action, without spilling blood. "Freedom is never voluntarily given by the oppressor; it must be demanded by the oppressed," King wrote in his letter.

On April 19, King and Abernathy were released on bond. Entertainer Harry Belafonte had organized a committee to raise bond money for protestors who were jailed. With King back, peaceful protests moved to the next level. From May 2 to 7, Birmingham police used fire hoses and dogs against a Children's Crusade in which more than one thousand youngsters were arrested. On May 8, protest leaders suspended the mass demonstrations.

On May 11, after a tentative settlement was reached, the Gaston Motel where King was staying and the home of King's brother were bombed. On May 13, federal troops arrived in Birmingham to ensure that the pact would be followed and vigilante violence would not be permitted.

The walls of segregation in Birmingham were crumbling, King said. "They are breaking down and falling down, because in this community more people have been willing to stand up for freedom and to go to jail for that freedom than in any city at any time in the United States of America."

The philosophy that King had articulated in his letter from Birmingham Jail triumphed when President Lyndon Johnson signed the Civil Rights Act in 1964, smashing Jim Crow laws.

Less than five years after the Birmingham campaign, Martin Luther King Jr. was dead. Coming to Memphis, Tennessee, in support of striking sanitation workers, King was standing on the balcony of the Lorraine Motel on April 4, 1968, when he was shot and killed.

FOUR GIRLS DIE IN BIRMINGHAM CHURCH BOMBING

1963

It was a normal Sunday morning at Sixteenth Street Baptist Church. Dressed in their best, the five young girls were giggling and primping in the church bathroom between morning services. It was Youth Day at the church and about four hundred people were present for the special program.

Suddenly a blast ripped through the Birmingham building. Thirty-inch stone and brick walls crumbled. Stained glass windows shattered. A clock in the main worship hall stopped ticking at 10:22.

And the five little girls in the basement bathroom were buried alive.

Someone had placed a box under the church stairs, just outside the women's bathroom. Inside the box was ten to fifteen sticks of dynamite. The explosion was so tremendous that it left a gaping hole in the church foundation, created a deep crater in the basement, blew a passing motorist out of his car, crushed parked automobiles like toys, and knocked out windows blocks away.

That Sunday, September 15, 1963, shook a nation, causing riots and marches in the aftermath. In the 1960s, Birmingham was one of the most racially divided cities in the United States. That same year, newly elected Governor George Wallace physically barred two African-American students from entering the University of Alabama. And Birmingham's commissioner of public safety, Eugene "Bull" Connor, sparked controversy with his use of fire hoses and attack dogs to disperse civil rights protesters. Racists had set off so many bombs in Birmingham's black neighborhoods that the city was nicknamed "Bombingham."

The church bombing followed a march on Washington in August where Martin Luther King Jr. delivered his famous "I Have a Dream" speech, an appeal for fairness and racial harmony. An estimated 250,000 people participated in the march but, obviously, the event and King's moving speech did not change some hearts.

The Sixteenth Street Baptist Church in downtown Birmingham was targeted because it was used as a meeting place for civil rights leaders such as Martin Luther King, Ralph Abernathy, and Fred Shuttlesworth. At the time, the attack was one of more than forty bombings in Birmingham that had gone unsolved—and the first to kill.

The wails of ambulances and police cars mixed with the cries and shouts of churchgoers, passersby, and family members of the buried five girls. More than twenty people were injured and taken to the hospital. Church minister Rev. John Cross grabbed a bullhorn and pleaded with people to leave the area immediately so rescue workers and police could do their job. Officials also worried that there might be another blast.

Dozens of survivors staggered around in the white dust and debris, their faces dripping blood from glass shards that blasted from shattered church windows. The only stained glass window that remained in its frame showed Jesus leading a group of little children. The face of Christ had been blown out.

The first body was pulled from the rubble less than two feet down. Then others were pulled forth, one by one, as though they had been clustered together and hugging when they were hit. Killed were Denise McNair, eleven; Carole Robertson, fourteen; Addie Mae Collins, fourteen; and Cynthia Wesley, fourteen. Amazingly, another girl—Addie Mae's twelve-year-old sister Sarah Collins—survived the dynamite explosion with glass embedded in her eyes. She was blinded in her right eye but lived.

Considered the peacemaker among her seven siblings, Addie Mae liked to sing in the church choir and sketch portraits. She and two of her sisters would go door to door after school to sell their mother's handmade aprons and potholders. Cynthia' father, Claude Wesley, was a volunteer in the neighborhood watch, patrolling his area nicknamed Dynamite Hill because of the frequent bombings. A petite girl, Cynthia liked to give backyard parties for her friends. Her father identified her body at the morgue by a ring that a friend had given her.

Denise was a Girl Scout who helped organize an annual neighborhood fundraiser to fight muscular dystrophy. Holding tea parties for her friends, Denise seemed destined to be a teacher or a doctor. An avid reader and honor roll student, Carole took tap, ballet, and modern jazz dance lessons at the local recreation center. She was part of the high school marching band and science club and a former choir member in her elementary school. Members of the Jack and Jill choir sang at Carole's funeral.

Speaking at the September 18 funeral services for Addie Mae, Denise, and Cynthia (Carole had a separate service), Martin Luther King said the children were "unoffending, innocent, and beautiful." Yet they were the victims of "one of the most vicious and tragic crimes perpetrated against humanity. . . . They are the martyred heroines of a holy crusade for freedom and human dignity."

But the answer to the bloodshed, King added, was not even more bloodshed. "We must not become bitter, nor must we harbor the desire to retaliate with violence," he said. "Somehow we must believe that the most misguided among them can learn to respect the dignity and the worth of all human personality."

After the bombing, chaos erupted in the streets, and more lives were claimed. Seven hours after the church blast, Johnny Brown Robinson was shot in the back by police. Officers said that sixteen-year-old Johnny had been throwing rocks in protest of the church bombing at white youths passing by in cars. When ordered by police to halt, Johnny ran. The officer said he fired over Johnny's head, but the wound was fatal.

Virgil Ware, thirteen, and his brother James, sixteen, were on their way home from their uncle's to pick up a bicycle so that both boys could have a newspaper route. The bike wasn't ready, so Virgil perched on the handlebars of his brother's bike with James pedaling, and they started down a country road. At the same time, two white boys—Michael Lee Farley and Larry Joe Sims—were going down the same road on their red motorbike. Both Eagle Scouts, the two had just come from a Ku Klux Klan rally and claimed they feared the two blacks were going to throw rocks at them. When the two Eagle Scouts passed, Michael told Larry to shoot. Pulling a revolver out of his pocket, Larry did just that. Two bullets struck Virgil in the cheek and the chest, killing him.

Arrested the next day, Michael and Larry were charged with murder. Pleading guilty, Michael got probation. Convicted by an all-white jury on a lesser charge of manslaughter, Larry was sentenced by a white judge to six months in a juvenile facility. The judge then reduced the sentence to probation.

The investigation into the Sixteenth Street Baptist Church bombing, however, seemed to be buried along with the four girls. Although Alabama State Police arrested Robert Chambliss, Charles Cagle, and John Hall later in September, the three were not charged in the bombing of the church. Instead, they were charged with illegally possessing dynamite, a misdemeanor, fined $100 each, and given 180-day jail sentences, which were suspended.

On May 13, 1965, the FBI under the direction of J. Edgar Hoover concluded the bombing was the work of former Ku Klux Klansmen Robert Chambliss, Bobby Frank Cherry, Herman Frank Cash, and Thomas E. Blanton Jr. Three years later, the FBI closed its investigation without filing charges.

The church bombing case was reopened in 1971 when a new Alabama attorney general, William Baxley, took office and vowed to bring the murderers to justice. On November 18, 1977, Chambliss was convicted of murder and sentenced to life in prison. He died in prison in 1985.

Herman Frank Cash was another prime suspect, but he died in 1994, before Baxley could compile a case against him. Thomas Blanton Jr. and Bobby Frank Cherry were changed with murder on May 17, 1999. Blanton was convicted of murder in May 2001 and sentenced to life in prison. Bobby Frank Cherry was convicted and sentenced to life in prison. He died in 2004.

The deaths of the children followed by the assassination of President John F. Kennedy two months later gave birth to a tide of grief and anger. The surge of emotional momentum helped ensure the passage of the 1964 Civil Rights Act.

Today, the Sixteenth Street Baptist Church still welcomes people. Built out of the bombed rubble with donations from around the world and reopened for services on June 7, 1964, the new church sanctuary has a stained-glass window with a black Christ, a gift from the children of Wales with money they gathered through a penny campaign.

Across the street from the church is the Birmingham Civil Rights Institute. The museum and archives are a reminder of the high price paid in the struggle for civil and human rights.

BLOODY SUNDAY

1965

It should have been a peaceful Sunday. Instead, the date of March 7, 1965, has gone down in history as "Bloody Sunday," a day when six hundred civil rights marchers attempted to walk across the Edmund Pettus Bridge over the Alabama River.

Attacked by state and local police with billy clubs and tear gas, the marchers were beaten back across the bridge. Fifty-six marchers were hospitalized, although only eighteen of them were hurt seriously enough to be kept overnight.

But the sight of people being clubbed amid a cloud of billowing tear gas shocked a watching nation. The hate-filled event galvanized sympathetic Americans, thousands of whom descended on Selma to start the march anew and march even a third time to support voting rights. The national publicity that the marches generated played a significant role in convincing the United States Congress to adopt the Voting Rights Act of 1965.

The Edmund Pettus Bridge became a symbol of the momentous changes taking place in Alabama and America. Today, the Selma to Montgomery National Historic Trail commemorates the events, people, and route of the 1965 voting rights marches in Alabama—on March 7, March 9, and March 21, 1965. The third march lasted five days and made it to Montgomery, fifty-one miles away. Established by Congress in 1996, the fifty-four-mile trail begins at the Brown Chapel A.M.E. Church in Selma and crosses the Edmund Pettus Bridge into Montgomery.

Back in 1961, the population of Alabama's Dallas County, with Selma as the county seat, was 57 percent black. But of the 15,000 blacks old enough to vote, only 130 were registered, mainly because the system was designed to keep blacks from voting. That represented less than 1 percent of the population. A group called the Dallas County Voters League attempted to correct that voting problem by registering black residents during the late 1950s and early 1960s. State and local officials, the Ku Klux Klan, and the White Citizens' Council blocked their efforts at every turn.

In early 1963, Bernard and Colia Lafayette, organizers of the Student Nonviolent Coordinating Committee, arrived in Selma to help in the voter registration project. In mid-June, Bernard was beaten and almost killed by Klansmen. SNCC organizers Prathia Hall and Worth Long carried on the work when the Lafayettes returned to school in the fall. Hall and Long were arrested, beaten, and threatened with death, but they continued the struggle to register blacks to vote.

When thirty-two black schoolteachers applied to register to vote, they were immediately fired by an all-white school board. Civil rights activists intensified their efforts after the Birmingham church bombing that killed four young black girls in September 1963. Students began sit-ins at Selma lunch counters where they were attacked and arrested. More than three hundred were arrested in two weeks of protests.

When October 7, 1963, rolled around, about three hundred Dallas County blacks lined up at the voter registration office on one of the two days per month that residents were allowed to go to the courthouse to apply to register to vote. SNCC members who tried to give water to the blacks waiting in line were arrested, as were those who held signs saying REGISTER TO VOTE. Despite waiting all day in the hot sun, only a few of the hundreds in line were permitted to fill out voter application forms. Most of those applications were denied.

On July 2, 1964, President Lyndon Johnson signed the Civil Rights Act of 1964 into law. Although it declared segregation illegal, Jim Crow laws still remained in effect. When blacks attempted to integrate Selma facilities, they were beaten and arrested.

On July 9, 1964, Judge James Hare issued an injunction making it illegal to even talk to more than two people at a time about civil rights or voter registration in Selma. The injunction suppressed public civil rights activity in Selma for the next six months. With civil rights activity blocked by Hare's injunction, the Dallas County Voters League (DCVL) requested the help of Dr. Martin Luther King Jr. and the Southern Christian Leadership Conference (SCLC).

The Selma Voting Rights Movement officially began on January 2, 1965, when King spoke in defiance of Hare's injunction to a meeting in Brown Chapel. Over the next few weeks, activists held voter registration drives and protests in Selma and adjacent counties.

Things came to a head on February 18, 1965, when Alabama State Trooper James Fowler shot a black man named Jimmie Lee Jackson in the stomach. Jackson died eight days later. He was said to have been protecting his mother and grandfather when they fled to a café after being attacked by troopers during a civil rights demonstration in Marion.

As a result, civil rights activists planned to march from Selma to Montgomery to ask Governor George Wallace if he had ordered state troopers to shoot during the demonstration in which Jackson was killed. They wanted Wallace to protect black registrants. Instead, Wallace denounced the march as a threat to public safety and vowed to prevent it from happening.

On March 7, 1965, about six hundred civil rights marchers headed east out of Selma on U.S. Highway 80. Led by John Lewis of SNCC and the Reverend Hosea Williams, the protest went smoothly until the marchers crossed the Edmund Pettis Bridge. On the other side, a wall of state troopers was waiting for them. The demonstrators were warned to immediately disband and return home. Then troopers attacked the marchers, knocking many to the ground and beating them with nightsticks. Troopers fired tear gas while other officers on horseback charged the crowd.

Brutal chaos ensued—captured on television cameras for all the world to see. Called "Bloody Sunday" for the violence that shocked viewers, the aborted march did just the opposite of what Wallace planned. Instead of derailing the civil rights movement, the bloody march drew even more supporters, both black and white.

Immediately after Bloody Sunday, King began organizing a second march for Tuesday, March 9, 1965. Hundreds of people responded to King's call to join the march. To prevent more violence, marchers sought to get a court order to prohibit police from interfering. Instead, Federal District Court Judge Frank Minis Johnson issued a restraining order preventing the march from taking place until he could have additional hearings later in the week.

But marchers were ready to go. As a compromise, SCLC decided to hold a "ceremonial" march that would cross the bridge but stop when ordered to do so in compliance with the injunction. On March 9, King led about 2,500 marchers to the Edmund Pettis Bridge where he held a short prayer session before turning the group back around. In doing so, King and the marchers obeyed the court order that prevented them from marching all the way to Montgomery. But not everyone was aware of King's plan, and not everyone agreed with it. In response, King asked marchers to stay in Selma until the injunction was lifted and another march could be held.

That evening, three white ministers who had come for the march were attacked and beaten with clubs outside a Selma restaurant. A white Unitarian Universalist minister from Boston, Reverend James Reeb, was the most severely injured. When Selma's public hospital refused to treat him, Reeb had to be taken two hours away to University Hospital in Birmingham where he died.

A week after Reeb's death, Judge Johnson ruled in favor of the protestors, saying the First Amendment guaranteed their right to march in protest. The third march was set for March 21. About eight thousand people assembled at Brown Chapel, including marchers of multiple faiths and races now walking under the protection of two thousand National Guard troops and federal marshals.

Under the terms of Johnson's order, the marchers were reduced to three hundred participants as they proceeded along the two-lane stretch of U.S. Highway 80 in Lowndes County. On March 22 and 23, protestors marched through chilling rain, walking ten to twelve miles a day and sleeping in muddy fields. On the morning of March 24, the march crossed into Montgomery County where the highway widened again to four lanes. As the march came closer to the city, more marchers joined the line.

On the final day, nearly 25,000 people marched to the steps of the State Capitol Building where King told them that the end of white supremacy was near. "I come to say to you this afternoon however difficult the moment, however frustrating the hour, it will not be long."

Later that night, a car with four Ku Klux Klan members overtook a car driven by Viola Liuzzo, a Detroit woman who had been ferrying marchers back to Selma from Montgomery. Liuzzo was shot and killed. Three of the Klansmen were indicted for the crime on the testimony of the fourth, an FBI informant. Although the men were acquitted of murder at their state court trials, they were convicted in December 1965 in Montgomery federal court.

The marches were credited with raising public awareness about segregation and the civil rights struggle. The marches also had a powerful effect in Washington. Presented by President Lyndon Johnson, the Voting Rights Act became a law on August 6, 1965. In Selma, more than seven thousand blacks were added to the voting rolls after passage of the act.

"What happened in Selma is part of a far larger movement which reaches into every section and state of America," Johnson said. "It is the effort of American Negroes to secure for themselves the full blessings of American life. Their cause must be our cause too, because it is not just Negroes but really it is all of us who must overcome the crippling legacy of bigotry and injustice. And we shall overcome."

LURLEEN WALLACE ELECTED GOVERNOR

1966

When the ballots were counted on November 4, 1966, Lurleen Wallace was elected the governor of Alabama in a landslide victory. It was the first time a woman had been elected to the state's highest office. That was an important historical milestone. But the most interesting fact about the event was not that Lurleen was the first woman governor. It was the man who was her husband.

Lurleen Wallace was married to George Wallace, who had been Alabama governor before she took the office. In fact, Lurleen had clearly been elected as a stand-in for her husband who was forbidden by state constitution to run for a second consecutive term. Lurleen let voters know right away that George would serve as her "special assistant," earning a dollar a year and making most of the important executive decisions.

What Lurleen didn't tell voters was that she was running for office with a terrible secret. The forty-year-old mother of four was dying of cancer. Only sixteen months after taking office, Lurleen was dead.

Alabamians genuinely mourned the loss of the state's first female governor and a woman they had come to love. Among her biggest accomplishments during her brief tenure were major increases in expenditures for mental health, including modernization of the state mental hospital and state school, plus a big funding increase for state parks. Lake Lurleen in central Alabama is named in her honor.

The first and so far only female governor in United States history to die in office, Lurleen lay in state in the capitol building on May 8, 1968. More than 21,000 mourners stood in line for up to five hours to pay their respects at her silver casket. Despite her emphatic request for a closed casket, George insisted that her body be on view with a glass bubble placed over the open part of the coffin. On the day of her funeral, all public and private schools, all state offices, and most businesses closed. Lurleen was buried in Greenwood Cemetery.

The woman who commanded such respect was born into a working class family on September 19, 1926, in Tuscaloosa, Alabama. Her father, Henry Morgan Burns, was a bargeman and crane operator. Her mother, Janie Estelle Burroughs, was a housewife. A tomboy, Lurleen loved fishing and roaming the countryside. Graduating early from Tuscaloosa County High School in 1942 after taking summer classes, the fifteen-year-old began working as a sales clerk in a local dime store. It was here that she met the man who would become her husband.

At twenty-four years of age, George had just finished law school at the University of Alabama and was waiting to be inducted into the armed services. A reputed ladies man, George was quickly attracted to the pretty green-eyed teen. Although he left for basic training, George returned to Tuscaloosa to recuperate from meningitis. While on furlough, he and Lurleen married on May 21, 1943. She was just sixteen years old.

The couple moved frequently to air bases as George's unit participated in the firebombing of Japan during World War II. After the war, the couple returned to Alabama where George almost immediately began running for office.

Born in the railroad town of Clio, Alabama, on August 25, 1919, George Corley Wallace Jr. was the son of George C. Wallace and Mozelle Smith. Young George grew up seeing his father and grandfather active in local politics. After earning his law degree, George volunteered for the armed services. During air force basic training, George contracted spinal meningitis, which ended his chances of being an airplane pilot. But he did serve under the command of General Curtis LeMay in the 58th Wing of the Twentieth Air Force and flew on nine missions. When the war was over, George set his eye on political office.

Too young to vote herself, Lurleen became the primary breadwinner for the family and often wrote campaign letters for her husband to sign. George quickly found political favor with voters, winning two terms in the state legislature and then state circuit judge for the Third Judicial District. Consumed with politics, George left home and children responsibilities to Lurleen. The couple had four children: Bobbi Jo, born in 1945; Peggy Sue, born in 1950; George Junior, born in 1951; and Janie Lee, born in 1961.

When George decided to run for governor in 1958, Lurleen became his able partner, although she was shy of crowds. After receiving the unwanted endorsement of the National Association for the Advancement of Colored People (NAACP) because he had denounced another candidate's ties to the Ku Klux Klan, George was soundly defeated in the Democratic primary.

When he ran again in the 1962 gubernatorial race, George set his strategy to appeal to segregationist sentiments in Alabama. He threatened to "stand in the schoolhouse door" to defy federal court orders on desegregation. As a result, George won the primary with the largest number of votes ever received by a gubernatorial candidate up to that time. He then went on to win the general election.

As first lady of Alabama in 1963, Lurleen opened the first floor of the governor's mansion to the public seven days a week. She also refused to serve alcoholic beverages at official functions.

During his first term from 1963 to 1967, George intervened in civil rights conflicts and heightened racial tensions that led to violence and death. Turning the Alabama State Patrol into the State Troopers under the command of Colonel Al Lingo, George outfitted his white-only force in uniforms with Confederate flag patches, steel helmets, and carbines. Brutal images of state troopers clubbing blacks and civil rights protestors, and turning flesh-ripping fire hoses on helpless people, flashed across the nation. When marchers started across the Edmond Pettus Bridge to demand equal rights, George ordered state troopers to respond, resulting in "Bloody Sunday."

But rather than maintain segregation, George's defiant actions helped lead to its demise. The 1965 Voting Rights Act was passed, changing Alabama's electorate by adding thousands of black voters to the rolls. However, George had won a national following with his fight against integration, prompting him to seek the 1964 Democratic Party nomination for president. Seeing that he couldn't defeat incumbent Lyndon Johnson, George backed out of the 1964 race and set his goal for the 1968 election.

Needing the high-profile office of governor to help support his upcoming presidential campaign, George tried to amend the 1901 Alabama Constitution to allow him to serve a second consecutive term. When it failed to pass the legislature, George turned to another option—to run his wife Lurleen for governor, knowing full well he would retain the power for himself.

Winning in a landslide, Lurleen set up her "chief advisor" George in an office across from hers in the capitol building. Staffers referred to them as Governor Lurleen and Governor George. Lurleen was inaugurated on January 16, 1967, but refused to have the traditional inaugural ball out of respect to Alabamians serving in Vietnam. And, although voters weren't aware of it, Lurleen knew her life was drawing to a close.

Evidence of cancer had first appeared during the cesarean delivery of her last child, Janie Lee, in 1961. As was common at the time, doctors told her husband, not her, that they had biopsied suspicious tissue. George withheld the information from his wife, and she didn't receive important medical treatment. When she was later diagnosed with uterine cancer in November 1965, Lurleen was devastated to learn that George had known four years earlier about the cancer.

After a hysterectomy and six weeks of radiation treatments, Lurleen ran for office. Only five months into her term, the cancer returned. Knowing the prognosis, Lurleen told her personal secretary in June 1967, "I won't be here a year from now."

Surgeons at the M. D. Anderson Clinic in Houston removed a tumor from her colon and began radiation treatments that were extremely difficult for the already frail Lurleen. Forbidden from being out of the state for more than twenty days at a time, Lurleen briefly appeared at her office and tried to keep up a semblance of an acting governor. She also joined George in California in November 1967 as he succeeded in getting on the state's ballot as an independent candidate for president.

In early January 1968, doctors found numerous tumors and recommended more radiation treatments. In February, surgeons performed a colostomy that left Lurleen bedridden. Throughout the spring of 1968, Lurleen underwent repeated operations to help deal with the excruciating pain and try to halt the cancer but to no avail. On April 13, 1968, Lurleen returned to the governor's mansion to die. George persistently lied to the press about her health, claiming in April 1968 that "she has won the fight" against cancer.

High school bands serenaded her with "Dixie" outside her window. Weighing less than eighty pounds, Lurleen was restricted to visits only from family and close friends. Off campaigning in Texas and Arkansas for most of that spring, George returned just in time to say goodbye to his wife. Surrounded by her family, Lurleen died on May 7, 1968. She was forty-one years old.

George Wallace went on to marry and divorce two more times and serve as Alabama governor, after successfully changing the state constitution ban against consecutive terms, for an unprecedented four terms from 1971 to 1979 and 1983 to 1987. He also launched four unsuccessful bids for the presidency. At a presidential race political rally on May 15, 1972, in a strip-mall parking lot in Laurel, Maryland, would-be assassin Arthur Bremer fired five shots into George. The assassination attempt left George paralyzed below the waist and in constant pain for the rest of his life.

Severely depressed, George became a born-again Christian and determined to come back fighting for his health and his political life. A year after the shooting, George stood strapped to a podium and addressed the Alabama legislature. Renouncing racism, George showed he was a changed man by crowning the first black homecoming queen at the University of Alabama. Running for reelection as governor in 1974, George won a quarter of all black-cast ballots for 65 percent of the vote, the largest margin ever posted in a primary.

In 1982, George carried 90 percent of the state's black electorate. He would have run again after his term was up, but his health was failing. After leaving office in January 1987, George accepted a symbolic position at Troy State University. After numerous hospitalizations, he died in Montgomery on September 13, 1998, and was buried in Greenwood Cemetery. His final resting place is next to Lurleen.

UNCLAIMED BAGGAGE CENTER

1970

Notice that lonely bag going round and round on the baggage claim track at the airport? No owner is in sight. What happens if nobody claims the luggage? Will it forever be homeless and its contents never again see the light of day?

An Alabama couple had the same questions. Only they decided to do something about it. Back in 1970, Doyle Owens was an insurance salesman when he approached two airlines and offered to buy the luggage no one had claimed. With a $300 loan from one of his grandfathers and a pickup truck from another grandfather, Owens was in business.

Of course, he had no idea what was in the suitcases or whether he could even sell the stuff or recoup his investment. But Owens was pleasantly surprised to find that the everyday and unusual items that travelers pack in their bags are definitely good sellers. The story goes that Owens sold all his first batch of merchandise in one day.

That's how Unclaimed Baggage Center in Scottsboro, Alabama, came to be. It is the only business in the nation that buys unclaimed baggage and cargo from major airlines and then resells it in a retail store. The business was founded in 1970 by Owens and his wife Susan.

At first, it was just a part-time business. The couple would travel to Atlanta to purchase unclaimed luggage and air cargo and items left on planes. Airlines usually hold unclaimed luggage for at least ninety days while searching for the owner. Airline baggage offices are often located near the baggage claim area where travelers can report missing baggage to officials. Generally, passengers fill out a claims form with a description of the lost items. Once found, airlines will deliver the recovered items to a home or hotel.

If the luggage isn't claimed, the items are stored in a warehouse and then sold contents unseen to Unclaimed Baggage Center. Most travelers are paid by the airline when they don't receive their luggage, so it is an incentive for airlines to match travelers with their luggage. And it's just good public relations.

Less than 1 percent of all bags are permanently misplaced by airlines. But that is still a huge inventory of suitcases and contents that find their way to the Alabama site. It adds up to more than 400,000 pieces of luggage annually. Unclaimed Baggage Center had grown so much that by 1978, Doyle and Susan Owens went full-time with the business and incorporated it in 1978. In 1995, the founders' son, Bryan Owens, took over the company.

Known as the "lost luggage capital of the world," Scottsboro attracts visitors from America and abroad to the Unclaimed Baggage Center that covers more than a city block. The 40,000-square-foot store displays about 7,000 items per day. Merchandise is neatly arranged as in a department store, such as the shoe department, electronics department, jewelry department, and so on. To help fuel shopping expeditions, the store also has an espresso café with Starbucks coffee and food from deli sandwiches to home-style dishes.

The Unclaimed Baggage Center campus added The Book Nook located in a recently renovated 111-year-old Southern home. The nook holds a large selection of art, collectibles and, of course, tons of books. The Annex has a constantly changing array of products including automotive items, crafts, textiles, cosmetics, household goods, and more.

When the luggage arrives at the store and is opened, the contents are sorted and either discarded, cleaned, and prepared for resale or donated to charity. About one third of the items are tossed, one third given to charity, and one third sold. More than half of the inventory is clothing, which is cleaned and prepared for sale at one of Alabama's largest laundry facilities, owned and operated by the Unclaimed Baggage Center. Luggage is seldom sold because it is usually worn out or damaged when it arrives.

On a regular basis, the center donates clothing, car seats, and strollers to foster care programs. Wheelchairs, walking aids, and eyeglasses go to aid programs in America and abroad. Clothing is sent to homeless shelters. About 16,000 eyeglasses are given to the Lions Club each year.

And for folks who might be curious—Unclaimed Baggage Center cannot help reunite travelers with their lost luggage. By the time UBC has gotten baggage, the airlines have already tried to find the original owners and three or four months have passed. Usually the bags have no identification on or in them. Once UBC gets the suitcases or items and puts them out for sale, they are usually quickly in the hands of new owners.

So what are some of the things that show up in unclaimed baggage? Think of all the many items that people take on trips: clothing, cameras, books, golf clubs, skis, skateboards, electric guitars, jewelry, souvenirs, kitchen items, tennis rackets, tents, sleeping bags, basketballs, fancy perfumes, gifts. It's an amazing array of the useful, beautiful, interesting, and downright strange.

Since folks often want to look their best whether they are traveling for vacation or business trips, they often take their very best clothing. That's why UBC stocks so much like-new and quality clothing and shoes.

Electronics, of course, are also a popular travel take-along. In addition to cameras and computers, folks seem to lose an amazing number of music players, clocks, and radios.

The center also handles lost and unclaimed cargo. This is merchandise normally sent from business to business, such as a manufacturer retailer or parts company manufacturer. Large unclaimed items are often shipped in big boxes or containers.

Wayward items include such unlikely things as a full suit of armor, wedding dresses, a three-hundred-year-old violin, a Gucci suitcase filled with ancient Egyptian artifacts, including a mummified falcon and shrunken head, a camera designed for NASA's Space Shuttle, a 40.95-carat natural emerald, a U.S. Navy $250,000 guidance system, two Lotus Élan racing bikes, and an ordinary sock containing a 5.8-carat diamond set in a platinum ring. In case you thought it was only a far-out scary movie plot, found slithering free amongst the baggage was an unclaimed live rattlesnake. On a plane.

The original Hoggle from the movie *Labyrinth* ended up unclaimed and now permanently resides in the Unclaimed Baggage Center Museum. Hoggle, in case you don't remember, was David Bowie's dwarf goblin in the 1986 film.

One lucky little girl got more than her mother paid for at Unclaimed Baggage Center when she bought her daughter a Barbie that had been left behind. When the girl yanked the head off her new doll, $500 in rolled bills spilled out of Barbie's body.

HANK AARON BECOMES
HOME-RUN KING

1974

It's the fourth inning. As he has countless times before, the baseball player steps to home plate, eyes the ball coming at him, takes a powerful swing, and sends the ball soaring.

A record crowd of 53,775 cheer wildly while cannons blast in celebration as the player runs the bases—first, second, third, all the way home. Although the outfielder nearly falls over the outfield wall reaching to catch the ball, it lands in the team bull pen.

And Henry "Hank" Aaron hits career home run number 715. The day is April 8, 1974. The date goes down in history as the day Aaron becomes "home-run king." He has beaten the record of 714 home runs set by the legendary Babe Ruth back in 1935.

Equally important, Aaron is a black man from Alabama who has fought immense racial prejudice to play his beloved sport and reach the record-setting pinnacle. The historic game took place in Atlanta, pitting Aaron's team of the Atlanta Braves against the Los Angeles Dodgers.

"What a marvelous moment for baseball; what a marvelous moment for Atlanta and the state of Georgia; what a marvelous moment for the country and the world," Dodgers broadcaster Vin Scully reported as Aaron rounded the bases, accompanied by two white college students who had darted from the stands to jog alongside the home-run hitter. Aaron's parents ran onto the field, too, as the fans roared.

"A black man is getting a standing ovation in the Deep South for breaking a record of an all-time baseball idol," Scully said. "And it is a great moment for all of us, and particularly for Henry Aaron. . . . And for the first time in a long time, that poker face of Aaron shows the tremendous strain and relief of what it must have been like to live with for the past several months."

Born February 5, 1934, in Mobile, Alabama, Henry Louis Aaron grew up in poverty in an area known as "Down the Bay." The third of eight children of Herbert and Estella Aaron, Aaron spent much of his childhood on a farm picking cotton. The backbreaking job, some say, helped form the extremely strong hands later used for hitting home runs.

Although his family couldn't afford to buy baseball equipment, young Henry learned to make do so that he could play the game. He practiced hitting bottle caps with sticks. He made balls of tightly wound rags and swatted them around the field. When he finally got a rubber ball, he used one of his mother's broomsticks to make it fly. Aaron grew up hitting cross-handed, which means that although he batted right-handed, he placed his left hand higher on the bat. At Mobile's Central High, he was a star football player, but it was baseball that won his heart. Jackie Robinson was his hero.

When he was just fifteen, Aaron tried out for the Brooklyn Dodgers in 1949. He didn't make the team, but he did join the Mobile Black Bears during his junior year in high school. An independent

Negro League team, the Black Bears paid $10 a game, but Aaron was thrilled to be playing.

After high school, Aaron joined another Negro League team, the Indianapolis Clowns, where he earned $200 a month. Only eighteen years old, Aaron helped his team win the 1952 Negro League World Series. His playing skills also caught the eye of the major leagues. Fielding offers from the Boston Braves and the New York Giants, Aaron went with the Giants, who bought his rights from the Clowns for $10,000.

On April 13, 1964, Aaron made his debut with the Braves, batting zero for five attempts that day. Ten days later, however, Aaron hit his first major league home run when the Braves squared off against the St. Louis Cardinals. No one knew it at the time, but that was the beginning of Aaron's journey to become home-run king.

Although he batted in only 13 home runs as a rookie, Aaron was steadily improving and by 1957, was named the National League Most Valuable Player. He had hit .322 with 44 home runs and 132 runs batted in. Aaron also led the Braves to the National League pennant that season. In the World Series against the Yankee, Aaron hit .393 with 3 home runs to defeat the Bronx Bombers in seven games.

In 1958, Aaron once again led the Braves to the World Series. This time, however, they lost to the Yankees. But Aaron had turned into a strong, steady, consistent power hitter. He hit thirty or more home runs in sixteen out of seventeen seasons from 1957 through 1973. In 1963, Aaron became the third player in history to hit thirty homers and steal thirty bases in a season.

But life was not easy for the baseball star. The 1950s were a time of racial segregation, particularly in the South. Because of Jim Crow laws, Aaron was often segregated when traveling with his team. While white players had their lodging and meals provided by the team, Aaron frequently could not eat or stay with the other players and had to make his own arrangements.

Following the 1965 season, the Milwaukee Braves moved to Atlanta, and Aaron kept racking up home runs. At the end of July in 1969, Aaron hit his 537th home run, passing legend Mickey Mantle. That put him in third place—behind Willie Mays and Babe Ruth.

In 1970, Aaron received his 3,000th hit, the first player ever to get 3,000 career hits. He now had five hundred career home runs. On April 1, 1971, he hit his six hundredth career home run. The 1972 season was shortened by a strike. But Aaron still managed to pass Willie Mays in home runs. That left only Babe Ruth.

In the 1973 season, fans waited to see if Aaron would pass the home-run record of Babe Ruth. Aaron was now thirty-nine years old, and some worried he might be losing his power. The year of 1973 ended with Aaron one run short of passing Babe Ruth. But setting that record wasn't the only thing on Aaron's mind. After his final game of the season, Aaron commented that he was only afraid that he might not live to see the 1974 season.

Aaron had received hate mail and death threats from people who didn't want a black man to shatter Babe Ruth's record. Even the media who provided positive press coverage of Aaron got threats. The editor of the *Atlanta Journal,* Lewis Grizzard, reported receiving numerous phone calls calling them "n----r lovers" for reporting on Aaron's victories. Grizzard also had an obituary prepared ahead of time for the baseball star, fearing that he might be murdered.

But Aaron received a flood of public support, too, in answer to the bigotry. Babe Ruth's widow, Claire Hodgson, announced that her husband himself would have cheered Aaron's victory. Newspaper cartoonist Charles Schulz satirized the anti-Aaron controversy in a series of *Peanuts* cartoon strips in August 1973, in which Lucy proclaims to Snoopy "Hank Aaron is a great player . . ."

Sports Illustrated stepped up to condemn what Aaron was going through. "Is this to be the year in which Aaron, at the age of thirty-nine, takes a moon walk above one of the most hallowed individual records in American sport . . . ? Or will it be remembered as the season in which Aaron, the most dignified of athletes, was besieged with hate mail and trapped by the cobwebs and goblins that lurk in baseball's attic?"

So the stage was set when the 1974 season started. A small controversy erupted when the Braves opened the season on the road in Cincinnati with a three-game series against the Cincinnati Reds. Braves management, of course, wanted Aaron to break the record in the home city of Atlanta. To ensure that, they were going to have Aaron sit out the first three games of the season. Baseball Commissioner Bowie Kuhn put a stop to that, ruling that Aaron had to play two games in the first series. Sure enough, Aaron tied Babe Ruth's record in his very first try at bat off Reds pitcher Jack Billingham. But Aaron did not hit another home run in the series.

On April 8, 1974, a record crowd showed up for the Atlanta game. In the fourth inning, Aaron stepped up to bat and hit career home run number 715 off Los Angeles Dodgers pitcher Al Downing.

A few months later, on October 5, 1974, Aaron hit his 733rd and final home run as a Brave. Thirty days later, the Braves traded Aaron to the Milwaukee Brewers for Roger Alexander and Dave May. On May 1, 1975, Aaron broke baseball's all-time RBI record previously held by Ruth with 2,217. That year, he also made the last of his twenty-one record-tying (with Stan Musial and Willie Mays) All-Star appearances. On July 20, 1976, Aaron hit his 755th and final home run at Milwaukee County Stadium off Dick Drago of the California Angels.

After retiring as a player, Aaron returned to Atlanta to serve in the Braves' front office. In September 2010, Aaron's refurbished childhood home was relocated to Hank Aaron Stadium in Mobile as the Hank Aaron Childhood Home and Museum.

"Hammerin'" Hank Aaron's home-run record would stand for thirty-three years until August 7, 2007, when Barry Bonds of the San Francisco Giants surpassed him.

ALABAMA FACTS AND TRIVIA

- Alabama's Robert Trent Jones Golf Trail is the world's largest golf-course construction project.

- America's first wave pool was built in 1970 at Point Mallard Park in Decatur.

- Cullman, known as the City of Churches, has more than two hundred churches within its city limits

- Alabama's name comes from a Native American tribe, the Alibamu.

- Founded in 1819 near the site of an early Indian village, Tuscaloosa occupies the highest navigable point on the Black Warrior River.

- A life-size statue of Hank Williams stands in Montgomery's Lister Park across from the City Auditorium, where Williams's funeral service took place.

- Currency issued in Louisiana before the Civil War ($10 notes bearing the word *dix,* French for the number ten) led to the South being called "Dixie Land" and gave Alabama her nickname, "Heart of Dixie."

- The first inhabitants of Alabama were Cherokee, Creek, Choctaw, and Chickasaw Indians.

- NASA's Marshall Space Flight Center in Huntsville built the first rocket to put humans on the moon.

- Dr. Martin Luther King Jr. began his ministerial career at the Dexter Avenue Baptist Church in Montgomery.

- The current Alabama Constitution (1901) is one of the longest in the United States, having over 100,000 words and more than seven hundred amendments.

- The Alabama Territory was established on March 3, 1817, by the same act that created the state of Mississippi.

- The first 911 call in the United States was made in Haleyville on February 16, 1968.

- The first city-wide trolley was built in Montgomery in 1886.

- Andalusia holds a world championship domino tournament and has done so annually since 1976. The largest payoff was over $450,000.

- John R. Cook, who founded Cook's Pest Control in Decatur, developed Cook's Natural Science Museum in the 1960s to share his private bug collection, which he used for employee training. Today, the five-thousand-square-foot museum, built in 1980, is open free to the public and is one of the largest animal and insect museums in the South.

- Singer Lionel Richie was born in Tuskegee, and the original members of The Commodores met as freshmen at the Tuskegee Institute now named Tuskegee University.

- Scottsboro is home to the Unclaimed Baggage Center, which buys and sells luggage lost by airlines.

- A Flomaton man set a world record when he cashed in his thirty-eight-year penny collection in 2005. Stored in four fifty-five-gallon and three twenty-gallon barrels, the pennies added up to $13,084.59, the largest recorded personal penny cash-in.

- DeSoto Caverns, located in Childersburg, was the first recorded cave in the United States. Cave graffiti was first discovered in the 1700s.

- Anniston is home to the country's largest office chair, standing at thirty-one feet tall.

- The first woman to serve as national security advisor, Condoleezza Rice was born in 1954 in Birmingham. A music teacher, her mother named her after the musical term *con dolcezza,* meaning to play "with sweetness."

- Magnolia Springs has the only all-water mail route in the continental United States, with daily delivery by boat.

- Montgomery is home to the world's first civilian flying school. Established in 1910 by Wilbur and Orville Wright, it was located at Maxwell Air Force Base.

- Clanton has one of the only two peach-shaped water towers in the country.

- Alabama is the only place in the world where all three components of steelmaking—iron ore, coal, and limestone—can be found within a thirty-mile radius.

- The longest jail sentence ever handed down in the United States was received in 1981 by Dudley Wayne Kyzer of Tuscaloosa. He received 10,000 years plus two life sentences for killing three people.

- Alabama marble is considered the purest and whitest in the world. It has been used in buildings such as the Lincoln Memorial in Washington, D.C.

- Alabama is home to four "moon trees." These trees grew from seeds that had accompanied astronaut Stuart Roosa on the January 1971 Apollo 14 mission.

- Montgomery has served as the state capital since 1846. Four previous capitals included St. Stephens, Huntsville, Cahaba, and Tuscaloosa.

- Dothan boasts the world's smallest city block. Located on a triangle of land where North Appletree, Museum, and Troy Streets intersect, the plot is barely big enough to hold a stop sign, yield sign, street sign, and monument proclaiming the block's honor.

- Alabama has sixty-seven counties.

- The state's worst day for tornadoes was March 21, 1932, when a series of twisters touched down across Alabama. Accounts vary, but some estimates put the human death toll at more than three hundred.

- The state's oldest public frame building is the Stagecoach Tavern built about 1821 in Mooresville, population fifty-nine. The building served as a post office before the current post office was built around 1840.

- In 1929, Wilbur Hutsell, track coach at Auburn University, hosted a "Cake Race" for freshmen to uncover new athletic talent and awarded cakes to the top twenty-five finishers. The

Cake Race tradition continues each year, but women race now, too.

- In 1917, fourteen-year-old Clyde Anderson opened a newspaper stand on a street corner in Florence to help support his family. Built from piano crates, his humble stand was the beginning of Books-A-Million, Inc., the third largest book retailer in the nation. The company is headquartered in Birmingham.

- Born in 1935 in Lanett, self-made millionaire Millard Fuller founded Habitat for Humanity in 1976. The goal of Habitat was to help people living in substandard housing become homeowners through no-interest mortgages, small down payments, and their own labor. Fuller received the Presidential Medal of Freedom in 1996.

- Spear hunter Eugene C. Morris opened a one-of-a-kind Spear Hunter Museum in Summerdale in 2006. The museum showcases his big-game trophies, including an African lioness, a spear collection, and other spear hunting-related memorabilia.

- The "World's Largest Peanut Boil" is held each Labor Day weekend in Luverne. Members of the Crenshaw County Shrine Club boil, bag, and sell tons of hot goobers.

- A brick dollhouse is built over the grave of Nadine Earles at Oakwood Cemetery in Lanett. The four-year-old died of diphtheria in 1933 before her father could finish building a promised dollhouse. The city allowed him to build it around her grave. Now residents maintain the furnished structure.

- At 112 feet tall, the tallest Ferris wheel in the Southeast twirls at The Wharf in Orange Beach.

- When William T. Mullen wouldn't quit drinking, his wife Mary threatened to let the world know. He didn't, so she did. Mullen died in 1863, and his wife erected a whiskey-bottle-shaped tombstone over his grave in Clayton.

- In 1704, the arrival of the ship *Pelican* was eagerly awaited in the French colony of Mobile. Its cargo was young French women to become wives to the colonists. The women were nicknamed the "Pelican Girls" or the "Cassette Girls" for the small trunks or cassettes that they carried.

- First held during World War II, the annual Hey Day at Auburn University in Auburn is a beloved tradition where students wear nametags and are encouraged to say "hey" to each other.

- Housed in a 1916 railroad depot, the Bessemer Hall of History has an unusual artifact: Adolf Hitler's typewriter.

- In 1540 Hernando de Soto traveled through much of what is now Alabama.

- On December 14, 1819, Alabama became the twenty-second state in the Union.

BIBLIOGRAPHY

America's First Mardi Gras (1703)
Mobile, personal visit and observations by the author.

Battle of Horseshoe Bend (1814)
Daviston, personal visit and observations by the author.
www.encyclopediaofalabama.org.

The Last Slave Ship (1860)
Mobile, personal visit and observations by the author.
Diouf, Sylviane. *Dreams of Africa in Alabama.* New York: Oxford
University Press, 2007.
Robertson, Natalie. *The Slave Ship* Clotilda. Westport,
Connecticut: Praeger Publishers, 2008.

Free State of Winston (1861)
Winston, personal visit and observations by the author.
www.encyclopediaofalabama.org.

Attack on Fort Morgan (1864)
Fort Morgan, personal visit and observations by the author.

Helen Keller Meets "The Miracle Worker" (1887)
Tuscumbia, personal visit and observations by the author.
Keller, Helen. *The Story of My Life.* New York: W.W. Norton &
Company, 2003.

Miller, Sarah. *Miss Spitfire.* New York: Simon & Schuster, 2007.

George Washington Carver Arrives at Tuskegee Institute (1896)
Tuskegee, personal visit and observations by the author.

MacLeod, Elizabeth. *George Washington Carver.* Tonawanda, New York: Kids Can Press, 2007.

Federer, William J. *George Washington Carver—His Life & Faith in His Own Words.* St. Louis: Amerisearch, Inc., 2003.

Books-A-Million Starts as Homemade Newsstand (1917)
Birmingham, personal visit and observations by the author.

Stern, William A. "Southern Fried Reading," *Forbes,* June 20, 1994.

Birmingham News archives.

Monk Begins Building Miniatures (1918)
Cullman, personal visit and observations by the author.

www.encyclopediaofalabama.org.

Boll Weevil Monument (1919)
Enterprise, personal visit and observations by the author.

www.encyclopediaofalabama.org.

The Poet of Tolstoy Park (1925)
Fairhope, personal visit and observations by the author.

Brewer, Sonny. *The Poet of Tolstoy Park.* New York: Ballantine Books, 2005.

The Scottsboro Boys (1931)
Anker, Daniel, et al. *Scottsboro: An American Tragedy.* DVD. American Experience Series. Alexandria, VA: PBS Home Video, 2005.

www.encyclopediaofalabama.org.

Goodman, James. *Stories of Scottsboro.* New York: Pantheon Books, 1994.

Norris, Clarence, and Sybil D. Washington. *The Last of the Scottsboro Boys.* New York: Putnam, 1978.

Coon Dog Graveyard (1937)

Tuscumbia, personal visit and observations by the author.

www.encyclopediaofalabama.org.

Tuskegee Airmen (1941)

Tuskegee, personal visit and observations by the author.

Earl, Sari. *Benjamin O. Davis Jr.* Edina, Minnesota: ABDO Publishing Company, 2010.

George, Linda, and Charles George. *The Tuskegee Airmen.* New York: Grolier Publishing, 2001.

Moye, J. Todd. *Freedom Flyers.* New York: Oxford University Press, 2010.

McKissack, Patricia, and Fredrick McKissack. *Red-Tail Angels.* New York: Walker and Company, 1995.

Rocket Man Comes to Alabama (1950)

Huntsville, personal visit and observations by the author.

Neufeld, Michael J. *Von Braun: Dreamer of Space, Engineer of War.* New York: Alfred A. Knopf, 2007.

www.encyclopediaofalabama.org.

Hank Williams's Funeral (1953)

Hank Williams Museum, personal visit and observations by the author.

Montgomery, personal visit and observations by the author.

Escott, Colin. *Hank Williams: The Biography.* Boston: Back Bay Books, 2004.

Hemphill, Paul. *Lovesick Blues: The Life of Hank Williams.* New York: The Penguin Group, 2005.

Meteorite Hits Woman (1954)

Alabama Museum of Natural History, personal visit and observations by the author.

Decatur Daily News, 1954 coverage of event.

www.encyclopediaofalabama.org.

Rosa Parks Refuses to Give Up Her Bus Seat (1955)

Rosa Parks Library and Museum, personal visit and observations by the author.

DeGezelle, Terri. *Rosa Parks and the Civil Rights Movement.* Chicago: Heinemann Library, 2008.

www.encyclopediaofalabama.org.

To Save a Mockingbird (1956)

Lee, Harper. *To Kill a Mockingbird.* New York: Harper Collins, 1960.

Lee, Harper. "Christmas to Me," *McCall's,* December, 1961.

Capote, Truman. *In Cold Blood.* New York: Random House, 1966.

Shields, Charles J. *Mockingbird: A Portrait of Harper Lee.* New York: Harvey Holt & Co., 2006.

www.encyclopediaofalabama.org.

Letter from Birmingham Jail (1963)

King Jr., Martin Luther. *The Autobiography of Martin Luther King Jr.* New York: Warner Books, 1998.

www.encyclopediaofalabama.org.

Four Girls Die in Birmingham Church Bombing (1963)

Birmingham, personal visit and observations by the author.

Branch, Taylor. *At Canaan's Edge.* New York: Simon & Schuster, 2006.

Brimmer, Larry Dane. *Birmingham Sunday.* Honesdale, Pa.: Boyds Mill Press, Inc., 2010.

Weatherford, Carole Boston. *Birmingham, 1963.* Honesdale, Pa.: Boyds Mill Press, Inc. 2007.

www.encyclopediaofalabama.org.

Bloody Sunday (1965)

Selma, personal visit and observations by the author.

www.encyclopediaofalabama.org.

Lurleen Wallace Elected Governor (1966)

Montgomery, personal visit and observations by the author.

www.encyclopediaofalabama.org.

Unclaimed Baggage Center (1970)

Scottsboro, personal visit and observations by the author.

www.encyclopediaofalabama.org.

Hank Aaron Becomes Home-run King (1974)

Mobile, personal visit and observations by the author.

Atlanta Constitution archives.

Grizzard, Lewis. *If I Ever Get Back to Georgia, I'm Gonna Nail My Feet to the Ground.* New York: Ballantine Books, 1997.

www.encyclopediaofalabama.org.

INDEX

ABOUT THE AUTHOR

The daughter of an old-time fiddle player, Jackie Sheckler Finch grew up listening to the music of Hank Williams and other legendary country musicians. Some of her earliest memories are hearing her father, Smiley Jack Poynter, playing music with his brothers and his band. Naturally, Alabama with its great musical heritage is one of Jackie's favorite places.

An award-winning journalist and photographer, Jackie has covered a wide array of topics—from birth to death with all the joy and sorrow in between. She has written for many publications and currently is the travel writer for a newspaper and the editor of two publications, along with being a freelance writer.

Jackie is also the author of twelve books, including *Insiders' Guide to Indianapolis, Insiders' Guide to Nashville, It Happened in Indiana,* and *Tennessee Off the Beaten Path,* and recently updated *Alabama Off the Beaten Path* (all published by Globe Pequot Press). She was named the Mark Twain Travel Writer of the Year by Midwest Travel Writers four times—in 1998, 2001, 2003, and 2006—and is also a member of The Society of American Travel Writers.

Jackie shares her country home with Pepper, resident guard dog and entertainer. One of her greatest joys is taking to the road to find the fascinating people and places that wait over the hill and around the next bend.